Country Home®

Quick

Country

Decorating

Country Home® Books
Des Moines, Iowa

COUNTRY HOME® BOOKS
An imprint of Meredith® Books

QUICK COUNTRY DECORATING
Editor: VICKI L. INGHAM
Associate Art Director: KEN CARLSON
Contributing Writer: DEBRA LANDWEHR FELTON
Illustrator: MICHAEL HALBERT
Copy Chief: CATHERINE HAMRICK
Copy and Production Editor: TERRI FREDRICKSON
Book Production Managers: PAM KVITNE, MARJORIE J. SCHENKELBERG
Contributing Copy Editor: CAROL BOKER
Contributing Proofreaders: JUDY FRIEDMAN, NANCY RUHLING, M. PEG SMITH
Indexer: SHARON DUFFY
Electronic Production Coordinator: PAULA FOREST
Editorial and Design Assistants: KAYE CHABOT, MARY LEE GAVIN, KAREN SCHIRM

MEREDITH® BOOKS
Editor in Chief: JAMES D. BLUME
Design Director: MATT STRELECKI
Managing Editor: GREGORY H. KAYKO
Executive Shelter Editor: DENISE L. CARINGER

Director, Retail Sales & Marketing: TERRY UNSWORTH
Director, Sales, Special Markets: RITA MCMULLEN
Director, Sales, Premiums: MICHAEL A. PETERSON
Director, Sales, Retail: TOM WIERZBICKI
Director, Sales, Home & Garden Centers: RAY WOLF
Director, Book Marketing: BRAD ELMITT
Director, Operations: GEORGE A. SUSRAL
Director, Production: DOUGLAS M. JOHNSTON
Vice President, General Manager: JAMIE L. MARTIN

COUNTRY HOME® MAGAZINE
Editor in Chief: CAROL SHEEHAN
Creative Director: MARY EMMERLING
Executive Editor: JEAN SCHISSEL NORMAN
Building/Special Projects Editor: MEREDITH LADIK

MEREDITH PUBLISHING GROUP
President, Publishing Group: CHRISTOPHER M. LITTLE
Vice President, Finance & Administration: MAX RUNCIMAN

MEREDITH CORPORATION
Chairman and Chief Executive Officer: WILLIAM T. KERR
Chairman of the Executive Committee: E. T. MEREDITH III

All of us at Country Home® Books are dedicated to providing you with information and ideas to enhance your home.
We welcome your comments and suggestions. Write to us at: Country Home®, Shelter Editorial Department,
1716 Locust St., Des Moines, IA 50309-3023.

If you would like to purchase any of our books, check wherever quality books are sold. Visit us at bhgbooks.com.

Cover Photograph: JEFF McNAMARA

Americans have always taken great pride in beautifying

their homes. Early settlers pieced together scraps of cloth, filled their pantry with the

fruits of their labor, and spun wool to brighten their plain homesteads—the bonus

side of keeping the household clothed, fed, and warm. These enterprising women

drew inspiration from the natural world in every season to fill the larder and decorate

the house. In celebration of this enduring country ingenuity, *Country Home® Quick Country Decorating* has been created as a

seasonal guide to making your own home cozier and more beautiful, using ideas that are simple, time-tested, inexpensive

to translate into reality, and appealing for every kind of country household.

In the comforting vocabulary of country, a "make-do" means making the most of what is at hand. The pages of *Quick*

Country Decorating are filled with suggestions for turning cast-offs, garden surplus, and salvage into personal expressions

of creativity to make the home pretty—and practical, too—throughout the year and the holidays. That dual philosophy

also is the watchword in every issue of *Country Home®* magazine, where the featured homes, gardens, and collections

resonate with a fresh new interpretation of country style. *Quick Country Decorating* is a distillation of our decorating

philosophy. We hope it serves as food for thought and inspiration as you go about applying some modern country

creativity to tackling your own home decorating projects.

Carol Sheehan

EDITOR IN CHIEF, *COUNTRY HOME®* MAGAZINE

{ Introduction }

A change of seasons always inspires me to freshen up things at home. I still remember how excited I was as a child to go up into the attic to bring out holiday decorations and to gather shells each summer along the eastern shore. Those simple activities have a way of creating wonderful memories. When my children were little, fall truly arrived when we visited the pumpkin fields. We always held a carving contest to choose the funniest face and the ugliest face. Today, at the first sign of spring, you'll find me reorganizing closets and cupboards with baskets and filling stoneware crocks with white tulips. Even after 30 years as a decorating editor, I'm always looking for new ways to bring each season's abundance home.

That's why the editors of *Country Home®* magazine created *Quick Country Decorating*. It's the perfect seasonal guidebook because it is filled with beautiful photographs, great tips, how-to help, and, of course, hundreds of quick ideas. You'll be tempted to jump into the first project you see, but take my advice: Start slowly by opening this book on a quiet day and savoring every single page.

When you're ready to get started, the country basics you need could be sitting on your mantel or stored inside an old pine cupboard. That's because, like me, you're probably a collector. I'm always rotating my collections, enjoying favorite pieces for a season, then putting them away for awhile. That's why I especially love the ideas that showcase the country antiques most of us have on hand.

These humble objects serve as perfect building blocks for creating clever storage, holding bouquets, arranging a wall display, or decorating a pumpkin. You'll want to dust off items you've stored away—old crocks, inexpensive bud vases, ironstone platters, and even a top hat (it's great for dressing up a pumpkin at Halloween!).

Many other quick country decorating essentials are yours for the finding. Walk a beach for shells, beach glass, and smooth rocks. Gather moss, twigs, evergreen boughs, bark, and pinecones on your next trek through the woods. Fill your trunk with boxes of apples and gourds, plus armloads of fresh-picked flowers from your local farmer's market or roadside stand.

I know it can be hard to make time for decorating when your days are jam-packed. That's why we designed this book to be simple to use. Each chapter outlines the basics for creating the projects and offers tips and ideas for ways to use other materials or to create variations on a theme. Look, too, for illustrations that show the easiest way to empty eggshells or how to make an apple garland.

Whether you sit down with family or gather friends for an afternoon of making projects, you'll be joining some of my favorite people who made this book possible. Much of the work you see on these pages is that of *Country Home®* magazine contributors James Cramer, Dean Johnson, and Matthew Mead. I'm always amazed by the inventive projects and beautiful photographs they produce. My friends and coworkers at *Country Home®,* especially Meredith Ladik and Jean Norman, had the wonderful idea of creating this book for you, turning a collection of ideas into a sourcebook you can refer to again and again. What makes me happiest, though, is knowing that this book not only shows you how to welcome a change in season, but also helps you build memories that last forever.

CREATIVE DIRECTOR, *COUNTRY HOME®* MAGAZINE

Spring

Enjoy freshly picked PANSIES in petite bouquets or press them to display under glass.

Celebrate spring with pastel-painted EASTER EGGS in country containers and as decorations.

ORGANIZE every room, using creative storage ideas to eliminate clutter and simplify your life.

FRESHEN UP with airy fabrics and furniture makeovers that bring new personality to your rooms.

For wreath instructions, see page 206.

{ Pansies }

PANSIES BRIDGE THE SEASONS FROM WINTER TO SPRING, their hardy blooms withstanding snow and late frosts to flower until summer heat sets in. They're perfect for decorating projects—the more you cut them, the more they'll blossom. Enjoy them in pots on the porch, indoors in arrangements, or pressed and displayed in Victorian-inspired accessories.

Decorating with Pansies

Both fresh-picked and dried, pansies brighten the home with vibrant color. 1. For an everyday celebration of spring, or as a special touch for guests, accent a mirror with a necklace of fresh pansies. Screw porcelain knobs into the corners of the frame and tie two strands of string to the knobs. Tuck long-stemmed pansies between the strings. The blossoms will stay fresh for two to three hours. Place containers of other pansies nearby to show off this flower's wide variety of colors. **2.** To enjoy flowers indefinitely, arrange dried blossoms in a vintage pot. (For silica-gel drying instructions, turn to page 14.) To make the arrangement, fill the pot with plastic foam or crumpled newspaper. Cover it with clumps of sphagnum moss, forming a gentle mound. Hot-glue dried blossoms to the moss until the top is completely covered. Use pansies of different colors or make the arrangement monochromatic to coordinate with the container.

1 2
3 4

5

Simple projects take advantage of the pansy's color and delicate shape.

1. Transform a tabletop with pressed pansies under glass. Use photocopies of vintage handwritten letters for a background. **2.** To make a Victorian-style "yard-long" wall hanging, have a glass company cut two pieces of glass 10×36 inches and drill holes in one long edge of each piece 12 inches from each end. Cut a piece of foam-core board a bit smaller than the glass; cover the foam core with light-color linen, gluing the edges on the back. Cut a piece of darker linen slightly smaller than the first; center it on the light linen, and use fabric glue to secure it. Glue dried pansies (see page 14 for drying instructions) to the darker linen. Sandwich the pansy board between the glass; thread heavy twine through the holes and knot the ends. Cover the edges of the glass with wide brown fabric tape, available at crafts stores. **3.** The Victorians displayed fresh pansies in pansy rings, which were wreath-shaped bowls. You can achieve a similar effect by filling a fluted or tube cake pan with long-stemmed pansies.

4. To decorate place settings, bundle pansies into nosegays and tie with ribbon. **5.** Look for opportunities to display pansies throughout a room: in baskets, in mint julep cups, and on shelves. To complement the flowers, purchase vintage pansy paintings and embroidered pillows at flea markets and antiques stores.

Because pansies are so delicate, they'll last longer if you display them in the simplest of ways. **1.** Stitch a slim pocket onto a pillow cover to hold the fresh flower of the day. Sew the pocket by hand, or use fusible web tape along the edges. Here, the flower is simply slipped into the pocket like a boutonniere. To prolong its life, insert the stem in a water vial (available from florist's shops and crafts stores), then tuck the vial into the pocket. **2.** The easiest way to enjoy pansies is to float the blossoms in water. Place them in a shallow container so you can look down into their faces. They'll stay fresh for days.

How to Dry Pansies

Preserve pansies by pressing them or by drying them in silica gel. Pressed pansies are best for decoupage projects; those dried in silica gel look almost fresh and can be used in arrangements and wreaths. To preserve flowers, pour silica gel crystals (from a crafts store) into a large plastic container to a depth of ½ inch. Pick flowers at their peak and pinch off the stems; lay them facedown on the silica gel, placing them 1 inch apart. Cover them with silica gel and add another layer of flowers. Repeat until the container is full, ending with silica gel. Cover the container and let the flowers dry for 7 to 10 days.

Displaying Miniature Flowers

Spring arrives with an abundance of tiny blossoms, such as snowdrops, grape hyacinth, and violets. Treat yourself to diminutive bouquets to enjoy up close. For display, try these ideas:

- Collect flea market bottles, such as vintage medicine, perfume, or flavoring bottles, to hold long-stem flowers.
- Tuck delicate stems into salt or sugar shakers with their lids still intact.
- Place short-stem flowers in custard cups, creamers or sugar bowls.

Edible pansies make a pretty addition to spring centerpieces and desserts. **1.** For a pansy-filled ice ring, fill a tube cake pan or circular mold with about ½ inch of distilled water. Arrange a layer of pansies facedown on the water and place the pan in the freezer. Let it freeze, then add more pansies and water; return the ring to the freezer until the water is frozen solid. To remove the ring from the pan, plunge it into hot water, then turn it out on a dish or platter. Fill the center with fresh fruit, salad, or a chilled dessert; garnish with fresh pansies. **2.** Turn sugar cookies into elegant springtime treats with pansies or their cousins, violets and Johnny-jump-ups. Use only organically-grown flowers; nursery and florist flowers aren't edible.

Pansy Sugar Cookies

⅓ cup butter or margarine
⅓ cup shortening
¾ cup sugar
1 teaspoon baking powder
1 egg
1 teaspoon vanilla
2 cups all-purpose flour
1 egg white
1 tablespoon water

1. Beat butter and shortening on medium to high speed for 30 seconds. Add sugar, baking powder, and dash *salt*. Beat until combined. Beat in egg and vanilla. Beat in as much flour as you can with mixer. Stir in remaining flour. Divide dough in half. If necessary, cover and chill dough for 3 hours or until easy to handle.
2. On a lightly floured surface, roll half at a time to ⅛ inch thick. Cut with a 2½-inch cookie cutter. Place on an ungreased cookie sheet. Bake in a 375° oven 7 to 8 minutes or until edges are firm and bottoms lightly brown. Cool on a rack.
3. Mix the egg white with 1 tablespoon water; brush on baked cookies. Place fresh flowers on cookies; brush with more egg-white mixture. Bake in a 325° oven for 5 minutes. Makes 36 to 48 cookies.

1

{ Easter Eggs }

SIGNS OF REBIRTH IN THE GARDEN are reason enough to celebrate spring indoors

and out. Easter eggs, one of the season's favorite symbols, represent spring's promise of

new life. For country-style accents that capture freshness and new beginnings,

fill your home with eggs decorated in soft, pretty pastels.

Eggs by the Dozen

Inexpensive and fun to decorate, eggs are best displayed in abundance. 1. To create a seasonal display on a cupboard, mantel, or sideboard, choose three glass containers of varying heights: Here, a citron yellow vaseline-glass compote, blown-glass vase, and Depression glass plate complement the hues of the painted eggs and bring their own sunny glow to the room. For the most even color, paint the eggs with latex paint or acrylic crafts paint rather than using dyes. Apply the paint with disposable sponge brushes to avoid leaving brush marks. To make painting easier, push wooden skewers into a block of plastic foam for a drying rack (see page 23). Weight the foam with a book if necessary. **2.** Dress up a potted topiary or houseplant for spring by mounding painted eggs around the base. (See page 23 for an easy way to empty the eggs of their contents.) Mound moss around the base of the plant so you'll have a foundation for nesting the eggs. To keep the eggs in place, glue them to each other with a dab of hot glue. Start with the first row at the rim of the container, and build up to the base of the plant.

1

Surprise friends and family with egg-filled buckets and bowls, hiding treats amid the straw. **1.** Create a country vignette on a chest or side table with straw-filled pails of eggs. Choose three sizes of galvanized tin pails (those shown originally were used to store lard in the pantry). Color-wash each pail with an alkyd enamel paint; after the paint dries, rub with steel wool to distress the surface. Fill the buckets with straw and color-coordinated painted eggs. **2.** If vintage ceramics are more your style, use pottery planters and bowls from the 1930s and 1940s as cottage-style Easter baskets. Fill the pottery with crumpled newspaper nearly to the rim, then cover the newspaper with moss. Bend a willow branch or other flexible twig to make a handle (just for show); insert the ends into the pot. Rest painted eggs, sugared almonds, and gift boxes on the moss; group the baskets on a sideboard or table for a spring centerpiece.

Sunny Side Up

Decorate and display Easter eggs inspired by classic country motifs.

- For one of country's favorite color schemes, paint eggs cheery yellow and mound them in blue and white bowls.
- Paint eggs mustard yellow, stripe them to mimic yellowware, and nest them in a vintage bowl.
- Paint eggs antique white or beige and pile them in ironstone bowls.

《 Painted in whisper-soft colors, eggs capture the freshness of spring. Emptied of their contents and coated with acrylic or latex paints, they make pleasing, although fragile, accessories for the season. 》

Easy Egg How-To

Decorating eggs is a folk art tradition. To empty eggs, try this technique—and plan to make lots of omelets or cakes.

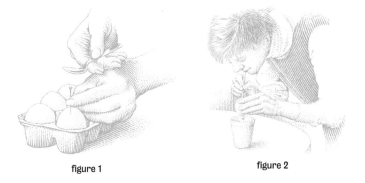

figure 1   figure 2

HOW TO EMPTY AN EGG

With the egg resting in the carton, place a dressmaker's pin on the top of one egg and tap it lightly with a spoon until the pin pierces the shell (see figure 1). Repeat this procedure to enlarge the hole until it's big enough to insert a wooden skewer. Push the skewer through the egg to break the yolk and pierce a hole in the opposite end. Hold the egg over a glass and place a drinking straw over the hole. Blow through the straw, pushing the contents of the egg into the glass (see figure 2). Gently wash the egg shell and let it air-dry.

HOW TO PAINT EGGS AND STRING A GARLAND

1. To paint the eggs, use flat latex paints or acrylic crafts paints rather than dyes; the paints will give more even coverage. Make a drying rack by pushing wooden skewers into a block of plastic foam, spacing the skewers 3 to 4 inches apart. Stand the block of foam on its side so the skewers are horizontal, then

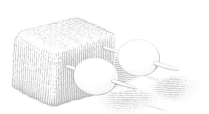

figure 3   figure 4

thread the eggs onto the skewers (see figure 3). Apply latex or acrylic paint with a disposable sponge brush. After the paint dries, thread the eggs onto ribbon or seam binding by pulling one end of the ribbon through each egg with a fine-gauge crochet hook (see figure 4). String about 24 eggs onto the ribbon, then knot the ribbon just below the first and last eggs. Add a bow from additional ribbon. Hang the garland from cup hooks in a door or window frame.

HOW TO SPECKLE EGGS

2. Speckled eggs are a delightful product of nature's creativity, but they can be hard to find. The good news is, you can make your own from a supermarket supply of chicken eggs. Empty the contents as directed (left), then coat the eggs with your favorite pale colors of spray paint. To speckle them, fleck dark raw-umber acrylic paint from a slightly damp brush or dribble it from a brush coated with color. Nest the finished eggs among straw or grass in a compote or candy container as a reminder that art can imitate life.

{ Organize }

OUR GRANDMOTHERS GREETED SPRING with a vigorous housecleaning: turning mattresses, beating dusty rugs, and washing all the windows. Mattresses still benefit from turning, and since we have a lot more stuff than our ancestors did, spring is a good time to clear out the clutter and get organized, too. With these ideas, find new ways to display and enjoy everyday treasures.

1   2

Pegs & Hooks

Country-style hangers help you get organized and keep necessities within easy reach. 1. In a bedroom, add wire hooks to a piece of architectural salvage like this Victorian-era pediment from a church. Check flea markets for old cast-iron hooks; these date to the 1860s. If they're wearing peeling paint, seal them with polyurethane or clear acrylic spray to avoid possible problems with lead. (Paint manufactured before the 1970s is likely to contain lead; if the paint is intact, it's not a health hazard, but dust from disintegrating paint is toxic.) **2.** Look for Shaker-style peg boards in decorating catalogs and home improvement centers. Install a row of pegs in the laundry room and hang bags made from old feed sacks to sort clothes for washing. **3.** Large cup hooks from a hardware store hold baskets above a desk. Fill the baskets with dried flowers or use them to organize papers, pencils, and office supplies.

Install hooks in bathrooms, kitchens, and near the back door so items you need often will be at your fingertips. **1.** For the bathroom, purchase large hooks at home centers, screw them to a 1×6 of the desired length, and hang near the tub or sink. Also check renovators' supply catalogs for reproduction hooks. **2.** Rest a vintage trellis near the back door to serve as a handy hat rack. Add flea market hooks, simply screwing them into the wood. **3.** Ash hooks reproduce those handcrafted by Amish farmers to hold horse harnesses; to achieve a similar effect, cut down walking canes and screw them to the wall. (For sources of reproduction hooks like these, see page 208.) **4.** Spruce up the kitchen with hooks made from forks. You'll find vintage utensils at flea markets and garage sales for as little as $1 each. Bend the handles around a dowel, using pliers if necessary, to create the desired curve. Use a power drill with a standard $\frac{3}{32}$-inch bit to bore a hole just below the tines of each fork; attach to the wall with a nail or screw. **5.** Scout flea markets for old hooks to hold bath supplies. If the metal is wearing a coat of worn paint, seal the painted surface with a coat of matte acrylic spray.

Hooked On Country

Shop flea markets and antiques stores for country-style hangers.

- In a workshop or sewing room, an antique pitchfork holds tools and supplies.
- Salvaged hooks are perfect for hanging garden tools and pails on the wall of your potting shed or garage.
- Collect hand-forged iron hooks of different shapes and sizes for useful and decorative displays.

1

2 3
4 5

Coming to Order

For a simple solution to too much clutter, enlist the help of classic country containers. 1. Use your collection of canning jars to organize all the items you've been tossing in your kitchen junk drawer. The jars make cookie cutters, pastry bag tips, and measuring spoons easy to locate, and they line up in style on a counter or windowsill. **2.** Outfit wire baskets (these are from old gym lockers) with white cotton liners and stack them on closet shelves to keep shoes, socks, and underwear tidy. To make a basket liner, hem the edges of a large fabric square and tuck it in the basket; turn the top edge to the outside. For a more fitted lining, like the ones shown here, stitch a fabric "box"; fold under and stitch the top edge to make a cuff. Allow for a slit at the front edge to go around the locker handle; run cording through the cuff to fit it to the basket. **3.** Serve up fresh hand towels by rolling them neatly and stacking them in a deep ironstone bowl or soup tureen. **4.** Used to carry milk or tools, flea market boxes with dividers and a wire handle can go to work in the kitchen holding rolled napkins or towels on the pantry shelf.

Try out containers in different rooms to find the perfect catchall for little necessities. **1.** Add under-shelf storage in your sewing room, pantry, or workshop by nailing or screwing the lids of widemouthed jars to the underside of the shelf. (Make sure the shelf is securely attached to the wall.) Look for old-fashioned candy jars at flea markets or antiques shops. **2.** Hang old wire baskets on the wall to store towels and bath oils. **3, 4.** Fill a rustic basket with extra rolls of toilet tissue and you'll know at a glance when it's time to buy more. The same goes for soaps; pile them in a stoneware bowl. **5.** To protect flatware, stitch a cutlery caddy. You'll need a 28-inch length of toweling (see page 208 for a source) and 12 inches of ribbon. Hem the ends of the fabric, then fold up 8 inches of one end. Mark the pockets for the silverware (allow extra room for the depth of the spoon bowls). Stitch through both thicknesses. Fold the free end over the pockets so the fold lies 3 inches above the pocket edge. Press. Stitch ribbon to each side.

Edging Shelves

To add creative country flair to shelf edges, embellish them with items from your favorite collections. 1. Check flea markets and yard sales for inexpensive linen towels that you won't mind cutting into strips. Use the borders to edge shelves, securing them in place with double-sided tape or pushpins. **2.** Other flea market finds that make good shelf trims include butter knives, old keys, rulers, bottle openers, clothespins, and wooden spoons. Attach them with hot glue, which can be peeled off when you're ready to change the look. **3.** Wooden drawer pulls are both decorative and functional, offering handy pegs for dish towels, pot holders, or even cooking utensils. Look for the pulls at a hardware store. Measure and mark their placement carefully; it's

essential that the knobs be precisely and evenly spaced. The knobs shown are 1½ inches apart. Use a drill to make starter holes for the knob screws.

Arranging Collections

Give yourself new views to enjoy with "shelfscapes" for spring. Keep the color scheme simple with one or two colors; add interest through a variety of sizes and shapes. Position the largest items first for a backdrop, then layer medium-size and small objects in front so the arrangement has depth. Overlap pieces to help lead your eye across the display, but remember to leave a little "negative space" (the space around an object) between some items so the grouping doesn't look crowded.

1

2
3

On Order

Whether you're cooking for two or twenty, you'll enjoy yourself more in a well-organized kitchen. Who wants to waste time hunting for the pastry cutter when you're in the middle of preparing a meal? To bring order—and beauty—to the kitchen, devise a clear-out-the-clutter plan.

First, remove from the counters anything you don't use at least every other day. Then sort must-have items by function and organize them in country-style containers: An old window box, for example, corrals assorted cutting boards against the far wall in this kitchen, and large crocks keep cooking utensils handy. If you have open

《 The kitchen is the heart of a country home. Make yours serene for spring by putting away anything you don't use often. On open shelves, arrange utilitarian objects as if they were art. 》

shelving, arrange bowls and platters so they're within easy reach for serving family meals. Edit your collection, however, and arrange the bowls, dishes, and platters to create a balanced composition (see page 32, "Arranging Collections," for tips). Otherwise, your open shelves could simply add to the feeling of clutter.

Look for spots to add hooks or pegs to put needed items at your fingertips. In this kitchen, a structural post acquires an added function as a pot rack with the installation of hooks. Cup hooks in the apron of the work table also help with storage.

If you have room for a work table, make your own country-style island: Attach industrial wheels to the legs of an old table that's a comfortable height for working.

{ Freshen Up }

NOW THAT YARD-SALE SEASON IS BACK, look for bargains you can transform into treasures, giving your rooms a fresh new look. Choose breezy curtains (or make them from inexpensive sheets) to let the sun shine in and stitch up easy slipcovers and gauzy tablecloths to lighten up rooms. A fresh coat of paint, preferably in ivory or white, can update tired-looking furniture and accessories, too.

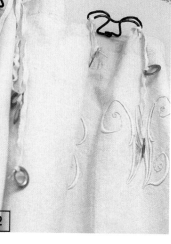

Window Dressing

Make a few additions to a bedroom or sitting area for a spring makeover. 1, 3. Plain panels of starched cotton create easy-going style. Install large grommets in the top corners of each panel and slip a metal curtain ring through the grommet. (Look for the metal curtain rings in decorating catalogs or the window-treatment section of home decorating shops.) Slip the curtain ring over a cup hook installed in the window frame. The rings make it easier to unhook one corner when you want to uncover the window. **2.** Another fuss-free way to hang curtains is to use old metal hooks. Thread clean white shoestrings through grommets or buttonholes in the curtain's top edge and tie the curtains to the hooks. Keep an eye out for interesting hooks at flea markets and thrift shops; you may find unusual shapes and sizes or even some with a worn patina that adds character to country windows and walls. Clean up rusty hooks by brushing off the loose rust with a stiff bristle brush, then spray with clear acrylic sealer to keep the rust from rubbing off on fabrics.

2  3

4

Creative details add fresh personality to window treatments. 1. To dress up plain curtains, string old wooden spools and beads (from a crafts store) on lengths of twine. **2.** Thread the twine through beads and spools as shown, bringing the twine through the third bead and back through the spools and beads. Cut the twine, leaving long tails to string through the grommets in the curtain's edge and tie a bow around the drapery pole. **3.** Turn a dish towel into a cafe curtain by stitching grosgrain-ribbon tabs along one long edge. To space tabs evenly, pin them at the edges and center first, then pin additional tabs halfway between the end and center ones. **4.** Tack the tabs with a few handstitches, then secure each one by sewing a button over the stitches. Hang the curtain from cup hooks screwed into the window sash and frame.

《 Layer on lightweight fabrics for spring and summer. Sheer and lacy tablecloths draped over a rod work well as curtains and valances. Striped cotton for the shower curtain adds a touch of soft color. 》

1

2 | 3

The lightest, airiest fabrics and laces accent windows without blocking the sun. **1.** For a romantic cottage-style treatment that requires no sewing, shop flea markets and yard sales for lace curtain panels and tablecloths. Mix and match them, then drape them over a curtain rod. Install an old-fashioned wooden finial on one side of the window frame at the middle or sash level; gather up the "curtains" and loop them over the finial. **2.** Look for vintage linens you can use as yard goods. Turning monogrammed or crochet-edged dresser scarves into shades, for example, creates a one-of-a-kind window dressing with character. A monogrammed dresser scarf fits neatly inside this window;

Roman-blind tape stitched along the sides lets you raise the shade in soft folds to welcome light and views. If you need extra privacy, add heavier curtains, leaving them open during the day to reveal the gauzy shade. **3.** Veil a window with a simple cafe curtain stitched from sheer fabric. Use fusible-web tape to attach four to six sheer pockets to the curtain. Then fill the pockets with pressed and dried pansies, ferns, and leaves or herbs, such as lavender and rosemary. (For drying and pressing instructions, see pages 14 and 102.) Hang the curtain from the rod using curtain clips, available at home decorating stores and through decorating catalogs; or use white or vintage wooden clothespins.

1 **2**

3

Fabric Softeners

Filmy fabric can change the whole mood of your dressing room or bedroom. 1. Gather cotton curtains with sheer ribbon embellished with silk flower petals. Check fabric stores for 2½- to 3-inch-wide sheer ribbon; at a crafts store, look for silk flowers with flat individual blooms that you can take apart. Tack or fabric-glue the individual flowers to the ribbon, attaching a seed bead at the center of

each. **2.** Use the same technique to add a feminine flourish to a sheer table covering. The organza tablecloth softens the look of a new metal table, but it also would freshen white wicker or painted wood. **3.** Bring out wire accessories to underscore a breezy feeling. Create an indoor window box with a wire plant shelf hung on the wall. A birdcage also introduces an airy look, and a wire basket or plant stand acquires new purpose holding toiletries. Use color to change the room's mood, too. Accessories, a rug, and fabrics in soft colors—tender yellow green, Russell-Wright pink, mint, and a range of yellows, from butter to daffodil—evoke the freshness of spring. (For product information, see page 208.)

Bring a pared-down look to the bathroom with humble country-style embellishments. **1.** Romance a tub with unlined curtains. Use ready-made curtain panels from a decorating shop. Or make your own from lengths of linen, muslin, or cotton: Hem the raw edges along the sides of each panel, then stitch a deep hem at the top and bottom. Leave an opening at each side on the top edge to slip the panel onto the curtain rod. Tie the end of each panel in a knot. Keep fluffy towels nearby in a big basket. Hang them to dry over a rustic clothes rack, assembled from branches secured with screws. **2.** For a shelf, lay a weathered wooden plank across the tub. Treat yourself to fresh flowers too; a plain white pitcher of daisies from the florist or daffodils from your own backyard will help you start your day with a smile.

《 Pamper yourself with simple luxuries—a pitcher of fresh flowers, a pine plank for a shelf, a basket of fluffy towels. Use chests of drawers or old work tables for storage with character. 》

Introduce softness to a room dominated by hard surfaces. **1.** For a gathered skirt, measure around the sink from wall to wall and double or triple that measurement; for the skirt's depth, measure from the sink to the floor and add 6 inches for top and bottom hems. Cut and piece widths of fabric to obtain the required skirt width. Turn under and stitch a 3-inch hem along one long edge. Make a second line of stitching ¾ inch from the hem stitching for a casing. Run ½-inch-wide elastic through the casing, adjusting the gathers to fit the sink. Stitch the elastic at each end to secure the gathers. Turn under and hem the bottom edge so the skirt clears the floor. Attach the skirt to the sink with hook-and-loop fastening tape.

2. To make a pleated skirt, piece fabric as needed to obtain a panel the length of the counter plus 12 inches (for two 3-inch-deep pleats) and ½ inch all around for seam allowances. Repeat for the lining. Stitch the lining and fabric together, right sides facing, with an opening for turning. Turn and press; slipstitch the opening. At the center, make two pleats. **3.** Tack the pleats with a few hand stitches, and attach the skirt to the counter's edge with hook-and-loop fastening tape.

Kitchen Facelift

In the 1920s, skirts hid plumbing and provided an attractive cover-up for cleaning supplies stored under the sink. If you have an old-fashioned kitchen sink, dress it up with a tab-top skirt hung on a tension rod secured between flanking cabinets.

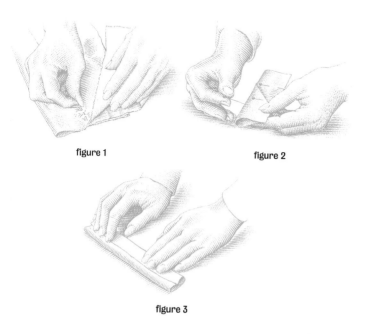

figure 1   figure 2

figure 3

HOW TO MAKE A PLEATED SKIRT

1. Measure the width of the sink opening and multiply that figure by 2½ to obtain the fabric width. Measure from the floor to the top of the opening to obtain the depth. Divide the width of the sink frame by 4 to determine the width of the box pleat; the pleat return will equal half of this measurement. Turn under and stitch a ½-inch hem at the bottom edge of the fabric. Make a 2-inch-deep hem at the top edge. With the right side of the fabric faceup, mark and pin the pleats. To secure them, fold the fabric for the left pleat over and stitch by hand or machine inside the fold, stitching an inch down the fold (see figure 1). Open the fabric back out; repeat for the right side.

To make the tabs, cut strips of fabric 4 inches wide and 4½ inches long. Pin and stitch the long sides together, right sides facing (see figure 2). Turn right side out and press so the

seam falls down the center of the tab (see figure 3). Fold the tab in half, seams together; stitch to the top hem, placing one tab at each end of the skirt and one inside each of the returns in the center pleats. Stitch a decorative fabric-covered button over the top of two pleats as shown. Slide the tabs onto the tension rod, then fit the rod behind the sink frame.

HOW TO MAKE A CHAIR COVER

2. Use linen toweling to make a tie-on dress for a straight-back chair (for a mail-order source of fabric, see page 208). To determine yardage, measure from the floor to the chair seat, across the seat, up the back, and down to the floor. Add 2 inches for hems. If necessary, take up excess width by folding along the inside edge of the decorative border. Pin and press,

2

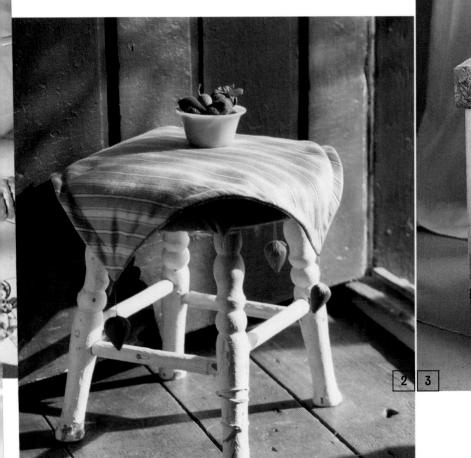

2 **3**

Makeovers

Celebrate yard-sale season by treating your finds to some new fabric and paint. 1. Tie old aprons over ladderback kitchen chairs for easy-as-pie country slipcovers. Leave the strings fairly loose so they won't pull when you sit on the chair. If the chairs are dull and worn, whitewash them first with a coat of thinned latex paint. **2.** Instead of replacing a stool cover, slipcover it with a kerchief. Cut two fabric squares large enough to drape over the stool top; cut a piece of thin quilt batting the same size. Place the fabric squares right sides together and lay the batting on top. Stitch with a ½-inch seam, leaving an opening for turning. Turn, slip-stitch the opening closed, and topstitch around the edges to make a flange. Weight the corners with old-fashioned dressmaker's pincushions, available from fabric stores. **3.** Soften the hard edges of flea market stools and benches with new or old fabric. Wrap thin quilt batting over the top and edges. Smooth your fabric over the batting and staple the fabric in place on the underside with a staple gun.

Fabric Options

New or old fabric in faded, tea-stained colors gives a vintage look. Try scraps of chenille for soft, nubby charm; '40s table linens for a retro feeling; toile for a more formal, sophisticated style; or ticking or gingham for down-home country simplicity.

{ Country Icons }
WOODEN BUCKET

Spring Ferns

1. Wooden buckets made of staves bound with heavy iron wire were the workhorses of farm life. Their versatility makes them just as useful for decorating indoors or out. For spring, tuck pots of ferns and primroses into the bucket to stand on a porch or in a shady garden bed. Use terra-cotta or plastic pots to raise the ferns and flowers to the rim of the bucket, and be sure to use saucers under the plants' pots to catch excess water so it doesn't damage the bucket.

1   2

Summer Corn

2. Fresh sweet corn is one of summer's tastiest pleasures. For a picnic or party, fill the wooden bucket with ears of corn, cleaned, partially shucked and nearly ready to drop into boiling water. Until it's time for cooking, the stacked corn makes an inviting party decoration.

Autumn Walks

3. As autumn brings a chill to the air, the tantalizing smell of wood smoke wafts across the countryside. In anticipation of building your first fire of the season, fill the bucket with kindling, pinecones, and rolled newspapers. In fact, the wooden bucket is so ideal as a fireside container, you might want to leave it on the hearth through fall into winter.

3 | 4

Winter Snacks

4. For a winter party, serve bread sticks in country style by arranging them in the bucket. Since the bucket is likely to be deeper than the bread sticks are tall, use bowls to raise a metal or plastic container to the desired height. Line the container with a kitchen towel, draping the towel over the bucket's edge.

Summer

Gather SHELLS to bring home the summer cottage look no matter where you live.

Step outdoors at DUSK for cricket concerts and firefly dances—nature's own Broadway show.

Breathe life into every room with FLOWERS fresh from the garden or farmer's market.

KICK BACK and relax with picnics, swimming, and sitting on the porch in your favorite rocker.

For wreath instructions, see page 206.

{ Shells }

SUMMER'S BEST SOUVENIRS ARE SHELLS, PEBBLES, AND SEA GLASS gathered at the beach. Decorating

with them becomes as easy as clustering them on a tray with pillar candles, but they're perfect for

more permanent projects, too. Even if you live miles from the nearest beach, bowls and baskets of

shells, sea glass, and pebbles placed on tables or shelves will remind you of salt air and sea breezes.

Simply Summery

Introduce beach-cottage accents with quick seaside projects.
1. Borrow an idea from museum displays and arrange your collection in a glass-top table, adding a journal or shell-identification book. Make your own display case from an old drawer and a picture frame fitted with glass or look for new versions of display tables in furniture shops. **2.** Craft a stony starfish to prop on a mantel or cupboard. Collect small white beach pebbles, wash them in cold water, and let them dry. Using five-minute epoxy, adhere the pebbles to a papier-mâché star (available from crafts stores). Position the pebbles so they follow the shape of the star, forming lines that meet in the center. Although the epoxy will set quickly, let the star dry overnight to make sure stones are secure. Then fill in between the pebbles with ready-mix plaster (also at crafts stores). While the plaster is still wet, remove any excess from the tops of the pebbles with a damp rag. Allow two days for the plaster to set.

Collect shells of the same type and size for uniform display and decoration. **1.** Make a summer birthday memorable with a ring of sea urchin candleholders around the cake. Select at least eight sea urchins of similar size. Trim tapers to fit the openings and insert them carefully into the fragile shells. **2.** Use *Turritella terebra* or similar long spiral shells for decorative bottle stoppers. **3.** If you're rich with sand dollars after years of collecting, use them to embellish a plain wood-frame mirror. Sort them by size (handle them carefully because they are so fragile) and look for a mirror frame that's almost as wide as the sand dollars so the delicate edges are protected from breakage. With wood glue, attach the sand dollars to the frame, overlapping them slightly. Glue smaller sand dollars over the points of overlap. Let the glue dry completely before you hang the mirror.

Even a casual summer supper will feel like a mini-vacation if you set the table with a centerpiece and accessories inspired by the sea. **1.** A white cotton tablecloth folded lengthwise dresses up the table without being formal. Scatter glass fishing-net floats on the cloth. **2.** For a centerpiece, arrange pillar candles on a platter, then mound shells around the edges and among the candles. **3.** Place sea glass in a drinking glass, then drop in stems of flowers for an easy arrangement.

Shell-Collecting Tips

For the best selection, go to the beach after a big storm or at low tide (local weather forecasts usually include tide times). Collect only dead shells and starfish—empty shells are a safe bet and won't need extensive cleaning. If you happen to dig up sand dollars still wearing their fuzzy brown coats, leave them alone—they will quickly rebury themselves in the wet sand. When shells dry, their color may change; to restore color and gloss, wipe them with mineral oil or baby oil, or use an acrylic spray. To bleach shells to a chalky white finish, mix 1 quart of water with 1 cup of bleach and soak shells for 30 minutes. Dry them in the sun for three hours. If you can't get to the beach, shop for shells at crafts stores or by mail order (see page 208).

Shell Game

Collecting shells is even more fun when you know how you will use them. As you head for the beach, keep these ideas in mind.

- Pick up small shells to surround a votive candle in a clear tumbler or vase.
- Look for large showy shells to set along a plate rail or the top of a window.
- Look for worn shells with holes that you can stitch to the edges of a tablecloth or the top of a plain curtain.

1 2
3

{ Dusk }

LONG SUMMER EVENINGS BECKON YOU OUTDOORS to enjoy the chorus of crickets and the gentle passage of twilight into night. Whether you're relaxing under the stars with a glass of iced tea or sharing barbecue with the neighbors, enhance the mood with candles and miniature white lights. Use items you have around the house as novel candleholders to give your gatherings country flair.

Outdoor Lighting

Bring the glow of candlelight and the twinkle of starlight to outdoor parties with these quick country ideas. **1.** For a beach party or picnic, cluster votive candles with rounded pebbles or stones. Use a permanent marker to write guests' names on the stones and arrange them as place cards. **2.** Turn a watering can into a candleholder for a garden party. Fill the can at least three-fourths full with sand to hold the candles firmly in place. Angle them away from each other so there's no danger of one candle melting another, then set the can on a surface that won't be damaged by dripping candle wax. Supplement the light with do-it-yourself hurricane lamps made by pairing goblets with vintage glass lampshades. Use inexpensive but heavy goblets with a bowl flat enough to let the votive candle rest securely inside. Scout garage sales and flea markets for glass shades; clear or frosted ones are best for softening the light, but milk glass or colored glass also produce pleasing effects.

1

As the sun goes down, group candles throughout the garden for an enchanting atmosphere. **1.** Create a floating garden in a washtub with round candles tucked inside water plants. **2.** Hang canning-jar lanterns from tree branches or porch beams. Twist heavy-gauge wire around the neck of the jar to make a handle. Pour a small amount of beach sand into the jar, then nestle a pillar candle into the sand. Use a long match to light the candles.

Getting the Most from Candles

Before lighting candles, trim wicks to about ¼ inch. Longer wicks produce more soot. To remove candle wax from votive candleholders, put the holders in the freezer for about two hours. The wax should pop right out. Or place the candleholders on a cookie sheet in a warm oven until the wax melts. Pour the wax into an old can and wipe the holders clean with paper towels. (Wear an oven mitt when handling the holders to protect your hands from burns.) If the old votive candles are scented, extend your enjoyment of the fragrance by pouring the melted wax into new votive cups or other molds. Insert a new wick, available at crafts stores. (Note that the color of such recycled wax may be grayer than the original candle.)

« **The magic of candlelight** is the glow-anywhere solution for after-dusk entertaining. Fill the yard with a variety of candles to add twinkling firefly-like lights everywhere. »

Turn glass vases and cylinders into creative night-lights. **1.** Create your own firefly show with little white Christmas lights and inexpensive florist's vases. Twist heavy-gauge wire around the neck of each vase and leave one end long enough to make a hook for hanging over the fence. Hang the vases at different heights, then string the Christmas lights along the fence, inserting enough lights inside each vase to create the firefly effect. **2, 3.** Assemble a sea-glass luminary with two glass cylinder vases in graduated sizes. Place a candle in the smaller vase and set it inside the larger container. Fill the space between the two with beach glass.

Candle Tips

Vintage flea market finds offer plenty of opportunities to display candles country style. Look for these secondhand winners.

- Antique flower holders called frogs are just the right size for slender tapers.
- A bucket-style sieve casts diffused light when votive candles are placed inside.
- A glass bowl shines with hollowed-out lemons filled with tea lights (small, flat votive-type candles in metal holders).

{ Flowers }

TWO OF THE LUXURIES OF COUNTRY LIFE ARE SPACE FOR A BIG FLOWER GARDEN and miles of roadsides

clothed in wildflowers and weeds. Treat yourself to an armload of hydrangeas or

bouquets of roses and wild grasses. To supplement your supply of flowers, frequent farmers'

markets, where you also can pick up fruits to use as unexpected accents.

Arrangements

Whether the arrangement is plain or fancy, roses breathe life and color into any room. 1. Let color guide your choice of companions: tiny unripened plums have an apricot blush that blends beautifully with the color of Oldtimer hybrid tea roses. Using a pitcher or similar container with an opening that's narrower than the container's body makes arranging easier; the opening works almost like your hand in holding a bunch of flowers—it holds the stems upright so you can more easily shape them into a pleasingly rounded bouquet. **2.** If you have a prolific rose bush, it's hard to beat the beauty of an urn filled with roses. To create a lush, full look, start at the rim of the vase, and cut stems short enough to position the flower faces at the rim or slightly below. Cut the remaining stems about the same length and insert them to create a mound. Position stems in a crisscross pattern as shown in the illustrations on page 83 so that each additional flower is supported by the stems already in place. Change the water every few days by placing the vase in the sink and letting lukewarm water run into it, flushing out the old water.

2

Keep arrangements uncomplicated to show off the flowers' beauty. **1.** Make a country statement by using vintage buttons to hold flower stems in clear glass vases. Fill a vase about two-thirds full of buttons. Add water, and carefully work in the flower stems. **2.** Pamper guests with a bouquet of garden flowers in the bedroom. Using a single kind of flower or flowering shrub, work with the natural lines of the branches, encouraging them to fall into a pleasing shape. (For more tips on arranging, see page 83.)

Taming Woody-Stemmed Plants

Use sharp pruning shears to cut woody stems, such as hydrangeas and roses, as well as fruiting branches of crabapples or immature apples, plums, or pears. Because the stem ends begin sealing over almost immediately, recut each stem on an angle when you bring the flowers indoors. Make a 2-inch-deep slit in the stem end before plunging the stems into warm water. To encourage roses to open more rapidly, put the stems in hot water. Strip the leaves off the part of the stem that will be below water; otherwise, they'll decay and shorten the life of the arrangement.

Rose Companions

To accent old roses in the garden, choose from these companions.

- Foxglove, clematis, pinks, and stocks provide color and form after the roses finish blooming.
- Foliage plants like sedum fill in after rambling roses fade.
- Roses on fences mix well with such vines as clematis and honeysuckle.

Show off colorful summer flowers by displaying them in classic neutral-color country containers. **1.** A stoneware crock makes a good container for a lavish bouquet of garden blossoms. Crumple chicken wire to fill the container and to help hold stems in place. Remove the leaves along the lower three-fourths of the stems; this prevents leaves from rotting in the water and lets you slip more stems into the arrangement. Allow vines or long stems to tumble down toward the tabletop in a graceful, cascading line. Also position flowers or leaves to spill over the container's rim. Insert flowers so the faces seem to radiate out from the center of the container, with some looking toward you, some down, some out, some up. This creates a feeling of motion that keeps the design interesting. **2.** Even simple bouquets of one kind of flower in a pitcher inject a splash of happy color and an exuberant feeling of life into summer rooms.

Summertime Facelift

The beauty of bouquets is that they require no color coordination, and they need not match their surroundings. Even if you have a specific color scheme, like the fresh white, blue, and yellow living room opposite, you can introduce new colors through flowers. Remember a few basics of the color wheel: Try a mix of cool colors, such as pinks and purples. To warm them up, add yellow and orange. Use foliage in a number of shades to fill in between blossoms and add cooling contrast.

Decorate your table with garden-fresh flowers and vegetables.

1, 2. The secret to this abundant bouquet is to line the basket with plastic water-filled drinking cups. The easiest way to keep so many stems securely in place is to fill the cups with florist's foam or crumpled chicken wire before adding the water. Alternatively, you can crisscross stems so they support each other (see page 83). **3.** Show off produce by using it as a centerpiece. Line up heads of cauliflower along the table for a cool green-and-white look. Or bring out an assortment of platters and cake stands and arrange yellow squash, green beans, and bell peppers on them for eye-catching color.

Long Live the Flowers

It's possible to keep flowers fresh for a week or more. For best results, follow these guidelines. Gather flowers in the early morning or early evening when they're not wilted by midday's strong sun. Carry a pail with you in the garden so you can plunge the stems directly into water as soon as you cut them. Let them stand in water in a cool, dark place overnight (this is called conditioning). Add florist's flower food to a bouquet, or add a few drops of bleach and 1 teaspoon of sugar to each quart of water. Replace the water every other day so flowers will look their best for as long as possible.

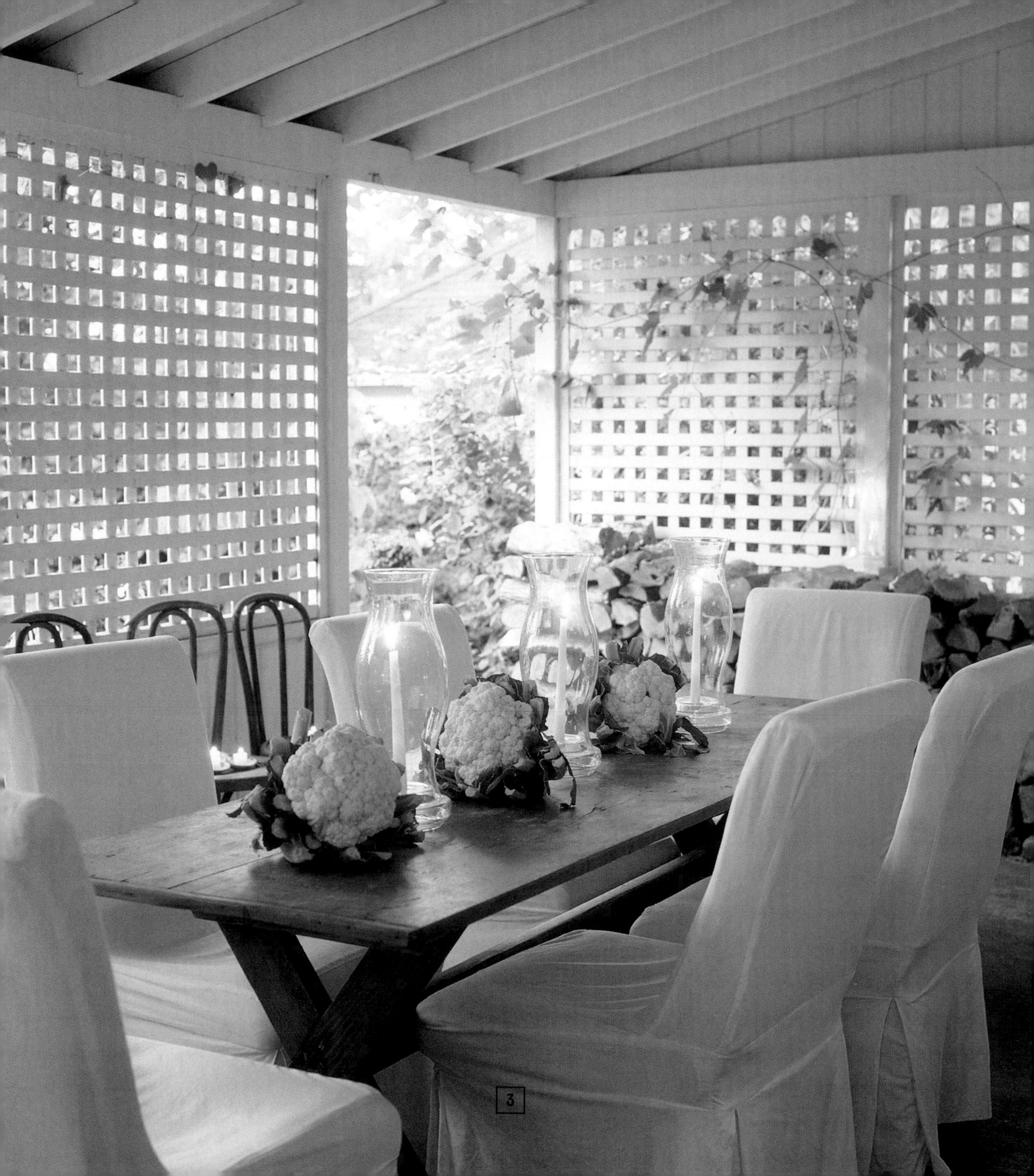
3

Combine summer perennials with roadside gleanings for a brilliant burst of color. 1. A syrup bucket makes a good country container, but if it's not watertight, insert a widemouthed jar to hold the bouquet. **2.** Instead of one big arrangement, make three small ones. The soft silver color of pewter sets off vibrant reds. This grouping includes Russell lupines, anemones, scabiosa, chocolate cosmos, pansies, roses, and rose foliage.

Flower Arranging 101

The easiest way to make flowers stay where you put them is to insert the stems in water-soaked floral foam, but they'll last longer if you simply place the stems in clean water.

BUILDING A FLOWER ARRANGEMENT

To arrange flowers using the stems to support each other, start with the flowers that establish the width of the arrangement, crisscrossing the stems **(see figure 1)**. Then position the tallest stem—for a vertical arrangement, it should be about 2½ times the height of the vase **(see figure 2)**. Add more stems as needed to bridge the gap between the highest and lowest flowers; fill in from side to side as well, creating a balanced (but not stiff) triangle **(see figure 3)**. Keep the rule of three in mind: flowers in three stages (bud, opening, and full-blown), three stem lengths (tall, medium, and short), and three shapes (spiky, rosette, and irregular). As you arrange, make sure you have a foreground, a background, and something that cascades over the side for a loose, graceful look.

figure 1

figure 2

figure 3

{ Kick Back }

WARM WEATHER AND LONG DAYS conspire to lure you outside to barbecue, garden, or just relax. Salute the season by bringing indoor furniture outside on a sunny day for a summer celebration. In the evenings, indulge in some "porching"—sitting on the porch and chatting with your neighbors.

Picnics

Make your Independence Day celebration a country event, complete with a flag, a farm table, and chairs set up by a river or lake.

1. Vintage pails are great for keeping cold and hot foods separate, or for carrying drinks and dry foods. Keep your eyes open at flea markets or yard sales for a twin pail like the one shown. **2.** Tempt swimmers to shore with a floating dessert tray. Rest a broad, linen-lined dough bowl on an inner tube and arrange treats on the towels. (Tie the tube to a line so it doesn't drift away.) **3.** Set up an old country table in the shade and layer it with square cloths arranged on the diagonal. Arrange a few wildflowers in drinking glasses or empty soda bottles for a simple centerpiece. To make the day especially easy, prepare a make-ahead menu of kabobs, grilled corn, broccoli salad, herbed potato salad, and a fresh blueberry or rhubarb pie. Keep a container of fresh-squeezed lemonade close at hand.

2 **3**

4

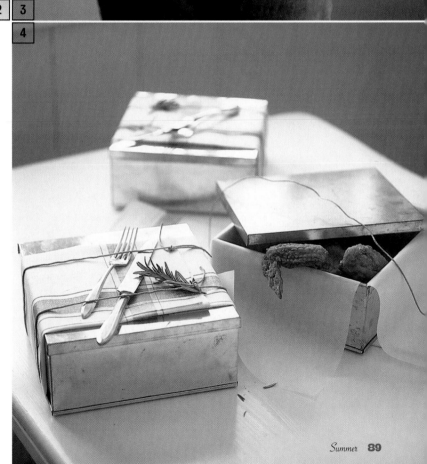

Country containers make great picnic carriers. 1. Pack food and drink in an old biscuit tin, with flea market cutlery and cloth towels that double as place mats or napkins. Tins like this, lithographed with a wicker design, were popular in the early 1900s. **2.** If you're only going out to the back porch, fill a small 1930s mixing bowl with chicken salad or pasta, top it with a matching plate, and tie it together with a tea towel. Look for glazed ceramics in summer colors at antiques shops. **3.** A large wicker tray is perfect for carrrying picnic paraphernalia. **4.** For a fresh take on a box lunch, pack individual lunches or suppers in old metal cracker boxes or biscuit tins. Wrap each tin with a linen or cotton tea towel (available at yard sales and flea markets), and tie with twine. Add a sprig of fresh herbs to contribute a light, summery fragrance.

Porches

D.G. Mitchell wrote in the 19th century, "A country house without a porch is like a man without an eyebrow." 1. A porch or backyard garden is the perfect spot for whimsy. Turn a broken child's chair into an inventive planter by wedging plastic pots into the frame where the seat used to be. **2.** Old metal pitchers can hold ferns or flowers with winsome charm. If the bottom is rusting out, so much the better; the holes will allow water to drain through the soil so plant roots don't rot. **3.** Carve out a spot on your back porch for a potting shed; an old bench holds terra-cotta pots until you're ready to use them, and a painted chest can keep potting soil and fertilizer dry and out of sight. Soften the supporting posts of a back porch with fast-growing annual vines; good climbers include morning glories, moonflowers, hyacinth-bean vine, cypress vine, wisteria, honeysuckle, Betty Corning clematis, birdhouse gourds, and New Dawn roses. Bring out a comfortable rocking chair so you can enjoy the view of your garden.

Make porches comfortable havens for relaxing and entertaining. 1. Choose washable cotton cases for plump pillows and cushions so you can toss them in the washing machine when they get dusty. If the sunlight is too strong on a screen porch, make panel curtains from canvas or cotton duck. Put grommets in the corners and along the top edge, or stitch plastic curtain rings to the edge. Hang the panels from cup hooks installed in the wood framing. **2.** The sun in the Southwest requires that you shade seating areas during the hottest part of the day. Over an open roof, lay straw matting from a building-supply store to filter harsh light. Hang long curtains made from canvas to provide even more shade. Use heavy-duty plastic or rust-proof metal curtain rings that will hold up under frequent use.
Pages 96–97: Swings and Adirondack chairs offer easy-care seating for country porches, but they'll be even more comfortable if you bring out oversize pillows to soften the backs and seats. Give wood furniture a fresh coat of glossy paint every summer to protect it from the weather. Hose off the pieces as needed during the season.

《 Make your porch a comfortable living space for the summer. Use cool, refreshing pastels to paint the floor and ceiling, and consider adding a ceiling fan to stir the air on the hottest days. 》

GLASS COMPOTE

Spring Greens

1. These elegant footed containers originally were used to serve—what else?—fruit compote, as well as nuts or sweets at the holidays or at dress-up dinner parties. For spring, use it to serve up a miniature plot of lawn. Grow your own grass in a tray of soil (see page 198 for instructions) or purchase wheat grass from a garden center. Cut handfuls of grass with sharp shears and stand it in the compote. A scant ¼ inch of water in the compote will keep the grass fresh for 3 days.

1 2

Summer Blues

2. Cool, calm, and contemplative, this centerpiece plays on the psychological effects of water, candlelight, and the color blue. Stand a pillar candle in the center of the compote; then fill the container with water and insert stems of blue anemones or other cool-color flowers. Cut the stems short so the flower faces rest on the rim of the compote, and use just enough flowers to ring the container. Too many flowers crowding in will interfere with the simplicity of bare stems in water.

Autumn Gathering

3. In the fall, assign butler duty to the compote, filling it with dinner napkins and silverware on a buffet. Guests may help themselves to one of each item after they've filled their plates. If you're having lots of people over, you might use a different compote for each utensil and another for the linens, just to help the line move more quickly. Line each compote with a freshly pressed vintage napkin to soften the clinking of silverware against glass.

| 3 | 4 |

Christmas Pomanders

4. For the holidays, fill the compote with fragrant pomanders. The pomanders are easy to make, using fresh oranges, whole cloves, and an embroidery needle. Use these examples as inspiration and let your imagination go when you decorate the oranges. With the embroidery needle, pierce the skin to make starter holes for the cloves. Outline monograms, lines, spirals, or curlicues. Then push a clove into each hole.

Autumn

Collect a BOUNTY of leaves and flowers in glorious colors and use them to make accessories.

HARVEST apples, gourds, and pumpkins for seasonal decorations to enjoy indoors and out.

TREAT yourself to festive fall sweets with cupcakes—just think of them as "baby cakes."

For wreath instructions, see page 207.

{ Bounty }

AUTUMN BRINGS A WEALTH OF COLOR in the pure, vivid hues of sugar maple, Bradford pear, sumac, and other trees. Surround yourself with that autumn glow by collecting leaves of all kinds and preserving their beauty through easy decorating projects.

Leaves

The easiest and most natural way to enjoy fall color is to press leaves or let them stand on their own. **1.** Arrange leaves in a bowl with nuts and sumac berries for a pleasing mix of souvenirs from a walk in the woods. To capture the best color, pick leaves from the tree at their peak or gather them as soon as they fall. Leaves should be dry and free of dew. For pressing, place them in an old telephone book or other book with absorbent paper (use a book that's not valuable, as leaves can stain the paper). Or layer leaves between sheets of newsprint and stack them under heavy books. Leave them for a week or two. Press green leaves, too, for refreshing contrast. Store extra pressed leaves in clear plastic sleeves and file them in a three-ring binder until you're ready to use them. **2.** Branches of autumn leaves make spectacular arrangements for a special event. Cut them just before the party and arrange them in crocks or buckets of warm water. To complete a harvest setting, gather pumpkins and gourds to fill country containers or rest on tabletops; fashion swags from inexpensive burlap to convey the texture of country.

2

Bring a sense of the season to the table with pressed and photocopied leaves.

1. Rim a charger with nuts, pressed leaves, and acorns to create a frame for an autumn place setting. Chargers made of rustic tin or pewter will give plates a primitive country look, but woven wicker suits the season, too. Top the chargers with harvest-colored plates. **2.** To make a coaster of photocopied leaf images, arrange pressed leaves of different shapes and colors on a sheet of paper, leaving a bit of space between them. Use a glue stick to secure the leaves to the paper, then make color copies of the sheet. With spray adhesive, attach copies to heavy paper, then cut out the leaves. Arrange as shown; use glue or spray adhesive to secure them to one another.

Larger than Life

When you photocopy leaves, enlarge a few by 200 percent or more to use for creative projects. For example, glue a single leaf image to heavy paper, then cut an opening in the center of the leaf to frame a snapshot or place card.

《Carry a small book or journal with you on leaf-collecting walks and slip your finds between the pages to begin the drying process immediately. When you get home, simply place the book under a heavier one. 》

Add depth to leaf projects by layering them on vintage-looking backdrops. **1.** To make harvest candleholders, start with clear drinking glasses (smooth, straight-sided ones are best). Photocopy old letters and fresh or pressed leaves. Cut out the leaves; trim the paper to fit the sides of the glass. Wrap the paper around the glass and secure the ends with glue, then glue on the leaf cutouts. Trim top and bottom edges with copper tape, available from crafts stores or stained-glass shops. Insert a votive candle. **2.** Create a leaf wall hanging, using a shadow box from a crafts store or frame shop. Line the back of the box with color-copied handwritten letters, using spray adhesive to secure them. Arrange pressed leaves, nuts, and berries; attach them with white crafts glue. **3.** To make a tray for silverware or napkins at an autumn buffet, start with an old, cracked platter (or use a wooden tray from a crafts store). Copy old handwritten letters on a color photocopier. Using decoupage medium or white glue thinned with water, glue the copied letters to the platter, overlapping them as needed. Wrap the paper over the edges to the back, and decoupage the back of the platter as well. Adhere leaves over the letters, then seal the entire platter with several coats of the decoupage medium or glue solution.

Branching Out

To add color to your home throughout the fall season, introduce pressed autumn leaves in a variety of ways.

- Photocopy them onto papers to use as gift wrap and tags.
- Place them under glass on a tabletop or under clear glass luncheon plates for individual settings.
- Glue them to a moss-covered wreath or to a mound of moss placed in a vintage pot.

3

Fall Changes

To shift a room's seasonal mood toward fall, use burnished colors and weighty accessories and let late-summer bouquets provide a warm focal point. For added impact, bring out heavy wooden candlesticks for the coffee table and mantel and create a new "mantelscape" for the season with layers of wood-framed pictures. The dark wood frames, an antique clock, and antler-inspired candelabra in the room shown all evoke a forest feeling; the

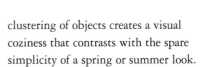

《 Give your rooms an autumn look by turning to nature for inspiration. The colors and textures of the forest—red and orange leaves and rich, brown bark—bring a warm, woodsy comfort indoors. 》

clustering of objects creates a visual coziness that contrasts with the spare simplicity of a spring or summer look.

Bring in armloads of flowers for bursts of fall color. Sunflowers, whether homegrown or purchased at a farmer's market, have lots of character. They are available in a surprising variety of forms and colors from sunny yellow to deep mahogany. For a bold sculptural effect, use large standard varieties alone in a chunky vase. For a fuller look, add small and medium-size flowers. Combine intense yellows with equally vivid reds to fire up plenty of visual heat in the room; add mahogany and purple accents for depth and interest. If you use florist's flowers, look for gladiolus and a variety of mums.

Once the flowers are arranged, replace the sisal rug with a wool Oriental; whip off summer slipcovers to store until next year.

2 3

Fall Flowers

The best harvest bouquets look abundant, yet casual and unfussy, as if you had assembled them in your hand and simply dropped them into a vase. 1. To help you position flowers where you want them, make a grid of florist's tape across the mouth of the container. The tape is waterproof and won't damage the vase as long as you remove it when the arrangement fades. **2.** Let the shape of the container guide your arrangement. A tall crock like the one shown suggests a tall spray that shoots up and out gracefully. If you use a fat, round pitcher, make your bouquet rounded and plump, too. Look for unusual materials for unexpected texture and shape, and be sure

to include stems that flow or cascade for a graceful effect. Here, pokeberries arch away from the backbone of the arrangement, which is defined by beautyberry and spikes of obedient plant. Phlox, China aster, and boltonia (which resembles wild asters) fill in empty spaces yet allow the design to be airy and loose. **3.** If you don't have florist's tape to make a grid, wedge a pliable, Y-shape twig into the mouth of the vase to guide the placement of flowers. This trick works best in small containers.

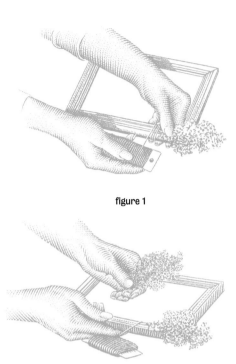

figure 1

figure 2

Autumn Edgings

Give yard sale platters and frames new life by edging them with elements of nature's fall bounty. 1. Reindeer moss, pinecones, nuts, berries, and dried leaves turn old plates and platters into clever substitutes for wreaths. Gather small cones and interesting twigs or pieces of grapevine from the woods; purchase dried salal leaves (also called lemonleaf) and reindeer moss from a floral supply shop or crafts store. Choose dishware with plain centers like those shown opposite, or look for plates that have designs painted in the center. Don't worry if plates have cracked or chipped edges; you'll be covering them up. Attach a plate hanger to the back. Then, using a hot-glue gun and glue sticks or thick white crafts glue, attach the dried leaves or reindeer moss to the edges of the plate or platter. Glue nuts, small cones, and tallow berries to the greenery base. Add grapevine cuttings or twigs to the back of the plate for a looser outline. Hang three or four in a grouping or display a single plate on a door. **2.** To frame old photos, souvenir postcards, or family portraits, cover old wooden frames with bundles of your favorite herbs.

HOW TO MAKE AN HERB FRAME

Assemble 3- to 4-inch-long sprigs of fresh or dried thyme into bundles of 8 to 10 sprigs each; wrap the stems with paddle wire (available at crafts stores or floral supply shops). Place one bundle on the frame so it extends just beyond the corner and secure it with paddle wire; don't cut the wire **(see figure 1)**. Lay a second bundle over the stems of the first, and wrap the wire around stems and frame **(see figure 2)**. Continue all the way around until the frame is covered.

Fragrant Frames

In addition to thyme, you can craft frames from other fresh herbs that will dry in place.

- Lamb's ears, complete with leaves and flower stalks, offer soft, fuzzy texture and a soft mossy green color.
- Baby's breath, German statice, and lavender provide delicate blossoms.
- Oregano, rosemary, and sage make great frames for the kitchen.

{ Harvest }

AUTUMN'S PLEASURES represent fruition: Apple trees white with flowers in spring now bear plump,

juicy fruits ready for picking. Pumpkins sown in early summer lie in the fields waiting

for Halloween, and gourds hang drying, waiting to be turned into clever decorations. Celebrate the

crisp air and blue-sky days of fall with a trip to the farmer's market to stock up on the bounty.

Apples & Gourds

Celebrate the abundance of the season with a generous tabletop display. **1.** Fill a brightly painted old washtub with dried gourds, apples, and berries. To reduce the number of gourds and apples you'll need, fill most of the washtub with crumpled newspaper or brown paper bags. Then arrange fruits and gourds on the crumpled paper, making sure you completely hide the paper. Tuck in pepperberries (available from crafts stores or floral supply shops) or clusters of red sumac berries; add nuts and acorns. If you place the arrangement indoors or in a protected spot on the porch, tuck in a few pressed leaves. **2.** For an easy-to-assemble centerpiece, start with a French breadboard, a long narrow platter, or a shallow basket. Alternate apples and dried gourds on the board, then tuck pressed leaves of various shapes and colors along the sides under the fruit. Use gourds that are all about the same size and shape to create a pleasing repeating rhythm along the table, but vary their positions as shown so the rhythm maintains interest.

2

1 | 2

Visit a local orchard for apple-picking and a last-of-the-season picnic. **1.** Be sure to follow the orchardist's instructions for plucking fruit properly so you don't damage the spurs for next year's crop. **2.** Anchor your picnic cloth to a table using apples tied with jute twine. Tie the twine around one apple stem, then run the twine along the length of the table and tie another apple at the opposite end. If the stem is too short, pierce the apple with an awl, run the twine through, and knot it under the apple. **3.** For a makeshift table, load a couple of sawhorses and a 4×8 sheet of plywood into a pickup truck. Pile in bales of hay for seats, and bring wool blankets for some padding over the hay. For the tablecloth, take along a roll of burlap.

Apple Dandies

Here are a few traditional apple favorites for cooking and eating fresh-picked from the tree.

- Braeburn: Sweet-tart and crunchy, these are good fresh and for sauce.
- Cortland: Tart and tangy, use them for pies and eating out of hand.
- Fuji: Juicy and crisp, they're great for sugar-free applesauce.

« **Greet autumn** with garlands made from the season's fruits. Drape these natural necklaces around windows or a door to dress your home in country style. »

Easy Harvest Garlands

Frame a porch or door with a swag of apples, leaves, or gourds to give an autumn accent to your house, barn, or garden shed.

MAKING FALL GARLANDS

1. Alternate apples and clusters of leaves along a length of twine. Use an awl or knitting needle to pierce through apples from side to side **(see figure 1)**. With a small crochet hook, pull twine through the hole in each apple, then knot the twine on each side to keep the apple in place **(see figure 2)**. Push branchlets of fresh autumn leaves into the apples near the twine holes, then hang the garland from cup hooks or small nails. **2.** Accent your garden shed or back porch with a swag of birdhouse gourds. Let gourds dry completely (this can take several months). Use an electric drill to make holes in the gourds at the "shoulders," near the top, as shown above. (Choose your drill bit based on the size of the twine you'll use for stringing the gourds.) Plan to alternate the gourds with a smaller item that will leave enough space between the gourds for them to hang freely. Dried seedpods, nutmeg, or walnuts (especially black walnuts still in the husk) are good options. Drill holes through these items, too. Arrange the gourds on the ground so the sizes graduate from the smallest at the ends to largest at the center. Then run heavy twine through the gourds and the spacer items, knotting the twine at each end of the garland to hold the gourds in place. Hang the garland over nails and tuck clusters of autumn leaves at the corners.

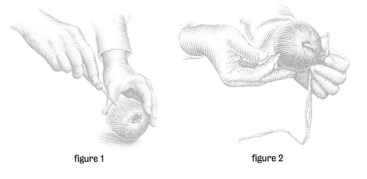

figure 1   figure 2

Harvest Table

The colors of harvest vegetables blend with country's warm hues, suggested by redware pottery and unpainted wood. Use antique dough bowls, shallow pottery bowls, or baskets to gather up an assortment of vegetables (turnips, rutabagas, yams, potatoes, onions) and winter squash, such as butternut, acorn, and spaghetti squash. Don't worry about arranging them formally. Simply pile everything in the container, being sure to include a variety of shapes and sizes. Place a few items on the table for a casual, unarranged look.

Pumpkins

Light up an outdoor party or indoor dinner with miniature pumpkins fitted with candles. Cut a hole just large enough to hold a tea light, scooping out the flesh so the candle edge is even with the opening. These pumpkin lights also bring a festive autumn look to a mantel.

Pumpkin Art

Forget the spooky faces. Give your jack-o'-lantern a country design that's rooted in history.

MAKING A WEEPING-WILLOW PUMPKIN

1. This Shaker weeping-willow pattern was a favorite for stenciling 200 years ago; stitched versions also appeared on embroidered mourning pictures in the 1800s. To make your weeping-willow pumpkin, cut around the stem to remove the top, then clean out the seeds and membrane. Enlarge the pattern as needed and trace it onto the pumpkin's surface with a pencil. Use a sharp knife to carve out the design, cutting just deep enough to expose the translucent flesh (don't cut all the way through; when you place a candle inside, the design will glow). **2.** Look to antique redware for inspiration to create pumpkins like these for decorating indoors or on the porch. Apply a coat of rusty red acrylic paint to standard orange pumpkins, then use white paint to draw linear designs like those found on redware jugs and pots.

Purposeful Pumpkins

Put painted and carved pumpkins to work with additional decorative duties:

- Insert candle spikes (antique or from a floral supply shop) as shown above.
- Use carved pumpkins as vases for fresh flowers and branches.
- Push a curl of wire into a mini-pumpkin to hold a photo.

{ Holidays }

FILL YOUR HOME WITH OLD-FASHIONED HOLIDAY SPIRIT. Homespun touches, such as fresh evergreens, fragrant narcissus, rosy apples, and handmade "snowballs," can dress up antiques for the season and imbue every room with a festive feeling. To get in the spirit of giving, spend a few winter afternoons making pretty gift wraps and homemade treats.

1 2

Decorations

Fashion a selection of trims from all-white materials to unify your holiday decor.

1, 2. Easy-to-make snowballs are elegant hung from the tree, attached to garlands, or nested in a bowl. To make a ready supply, start with plastic foam balls (from a crafts store), plaster mix, 12-gauge wire, pearlescent white spray paint, and white glitter. Push a length of wire almost all the way through a foam ball. With needle-nose pliers, curl the end of the wire. Mix plaster according to the manufacturer's directions until it's the consistency of thick frosting. (Add water as you work to keep the plaster from getting too hard and thick.) Dip the ball into the plaster; spread plaster evenly over the ball. Hang the ball to dry for 24 hours, spreading newspapers underneath to catch drips. Spray with paint; sprinkle glitter into the wet paint. **3.** To bring a snow-kissed look to your room, skirt a table with a cotton blanket, knotting corners to take up the excess. Make an overskirt by stitching snowflakes cut from white flannel to a purchased tablecloth or throw.

3

The glories of the garden persist through the holidays when you gather natural touches of red and green from your own backyard.
1. Turn the holiday spotlight on a bureau with containers of candy canes and nuts and a pot of blooming amaryllis or poinsettias. Add a pinecone swag or a garland of greenery to accent the paintings, plates, or mirrors you have hanging above the bureau year-round. **2.** Create a mossy Christmas garden by filling miniature terra-cotta pots with garden soil and topping the soil with pads of moss. Rest the pots on pillows of moss mounded in a shallow bowl or platter, and tuck bits of evergreens and red berries among them for contrasting texture and color. Mist the moss occasionally to keep it green throughout the holiday season. **3.** Broadleaf evergreens, such as mountain laurel and magnolia, provide a refreshing departure from needle-leaved evergreens for tucking around ornaments. Rinse the leaves and buff them with a soft cloth to enhance their naturally glossy surfaces. Fill glass containers with silver ornaments and arrange them on the mantel with packages wrapped in white.

Nuts are traditional stocking stuffers, but they serve more decorative purposes, too. **1.** Fill a shallow bowl with mixed nuts in the shell and add spicy pomanders for fragrance and color. To make the pomanders, use an embroidery needle to pierce holes in the skin of an orange, making lines, spirals, or other designs. Press cloves into the holes. For tiny pomanders, use kumquats, inserting cloves in a random pattern. Added to the bowl of oranges and nuts, the kumquats offer a contrasting scale that makes the display more intriguing. Or mound them in their own miniature container for a delightful little decoration. **2.** Guide guests to your door with a country-style star made of pecans and hazelnuts still in the shell. To make the star, follow the directions at right.

Holiday Star

Pecans and hazelnuts cover a plywood base in a subtle mosaic pattern that's edged with sprigs of boxwood.

HOW TO MAKE A STAR

Determine how tall you want the star to be (18 inches, for example). Divide that number by 2.66 to obtain the height of one arm of the star (from its tip to the center of its base). Divide that number by three to obtain half the width of the base. Mark that measurement on the long edge of a piece of paper, then accordion-fold the paper until you have five folds (**see figure 1**).

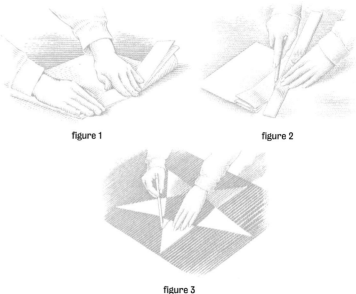

figure 1   figure 2

figure 3

Mark the height of the star on one fold; use a crafts knife to cut through all layers (**see figure 2**). Unfold the triangles and arrange them on the plywood with corners touching (**see figure 3**). Draw around the star on the plywood; cut it out, using a jigsaw or scrollsaw. Glue a row of hazelnuts around the outside edge. (Although you can use hot-melt adhesive, five-minute epoxy will give a sturdier, longer-lasting bond.) Fill in each triangle with pecans, aligned as shown. Fill in the center of the star with hazelnuts. Tuck sprigs of boxwood around the edges, slipping the stems between the nuts to secure them.

Trees

With some imagination, you can present your tree in an unexpected stand that has real country flair. 1. A roll of antique or new garden edging from a garden center makes a decorative base for a slender, primitive-style tree. Set the tree in a pot of soil or pea gravel, then cover the soil with moss before inserting the pot into the center of the wire roll. Trim the tree with lightweight garlands. **2.** If you don't have room for a big tree in your house, a petite tree in an old enamelware breadbox may be just right. Buy a small live tree with a root ball wrapped in burlap or potted in a plastic container to slip into the breadbox. Or use a freshly cut sapling; place its trunk in a watertight container and hold it upright by pouring pea gravel around the trunk. Slip the waterproof container into the breadbox, then add water. Place the tree on a tabletop or chest.

Enjoying Live Trees

- Place live burlapped trees in weathered terra-cotta pots to display on a windowsill. Cover the root balls with moss, then arrange festive red pears or pomegranates around the trunks.
- Use live trees to frame a front door. Leaving their root balls wrapped in burlap, place them on each side of the door or along a front porch.
- Give tiny trees as holiday gifts. Group several, planted in rustic pots, in a vintage milk carrier or wooden box.

《 **Adopt small old-fashioned-looking trees** in many shapes and sizes, then place them in unexpected spots, such as the kitchen, garden room, or guest room.

Christmas tree stands don't have to be traditional. Search flea markets or thrift stores for unusual containers that add to a tree's country expression. **1.** Turn a kitchen stool upside down and wedge a rusted metal bucket between the legs to hold a small tree. **2.** An antique English shopping basket, apple basket, or woven hamper offers lots of charm and makes a tree easy to move from room to room. A well-shaped tree in an unusual container needs little more than a fluffy bow and a star to look well-dressed. To keep the tree fresh, insert the trunk in a waterproof container inside the basket, holding the tree upright with pea gravel. **3.** Display a row of saplings in an antique dry sink. If you use live trees, insert the nursery containers inside terra-cotta pots, then mound nuts or moss over the soil for extra decoration. If you prefer to use cut saplings, insert the trunks into wet florist's foam in the pots and cover the foam with nuts, star anise, and clove-studded orange pomanders. Arrange the pots inside a box so you can move the grouping to the dining table for a centerpiece or to a buffet table for a party.

1 2

Packages

Packages are more fun to give and receive when they come in wraps that are gifts in themselves. 1. Dress up a plain brown package with raffia and a monogram made from cranberries. String the cranberries on crafts wire, then shape the first letter of the recipient's name. **2.** Give two gifts in one: a dozen or so of your best homemade cookies, presented in an ironstone covered dish. Run ribbon under the dish and through the handles and tie it in a big bow on top. **3.** Red ribbon against red paper looks brilliantly festive, especially when it's accented with green bay leaves and red pepperberries glued to the ribbon. Attach an antique Christmas postcard for a gift card that's also a keepsake. To wrap a gift that's an awkward shape or size, use a vintage towel or embroider a design in red on new coarsely woven toweling. Or work a cross-stitch design in red on Aida cloth.

Quick Cards

Turn handmade greeting cards into miniature gifts by adding something extra to every one.

1. To surprise your favorite gardener, send a card that's a miniature flowerpot. Use spray adhesive to glue a piece of red origami paper to heavy white paper. Cut a peat pot in half and paint it white, then glue it to the red paper. Tuck in a sprig of fresh rosemary and add a twine bow. To display greeting cards, slip them between the teeth of vintage or new flower frogs. **2.** Photocopy old letters on a color copier, then fold the paper like an accordion. Draw half of a tree on the fold; cut it out paper-doll style. Cut two slits in the center of each tree and slip in a sprig of your favorite herb. Write a message on the back or add a gift tag.

Foods fried in oil are a holiday tradition, recalling the miracle of Hanukkah, when a single day's supply of fresh oil for the Temple lasted eight days. **1.** According to food historian Alice Ross, in regions where Jews could raise dairy animals, cheese pancakes became part of the traditional meal. Alice serves them as dessert with her own homemade grape conserve. **2.** In Eastern Europe and Russia, however, the soil was too poor to support dairy animals but would produce potatoes, so potato latkes became a Hanukkah tradition. Note that according to Jewish dietary laws, foods containing dairy products may not be served alongside or following a meal that features meat.

Grape Conserve

3½	pounds ripe Concord grapes or use 4⅔ cups juice
1	lemon, rind and pulp (¼ cup juice)
1	orange, rind and pulp (⅓ cup juice)
1	package (1¾-ounce) powdered fruit pectin
½	teaspoon margarine
7	cups sugar
½	cup sultanas or golden raisins
½	cup walnuts, almonds, or pistachio nuts

1. Rinse grapes. Remove stems. Place in a large saucepan and crush with a potato masher. Add ½ cup *water* and bring to a boil over medium-high heat. Cover. Lower heat and simmer, covered, 10 minutes.

2. Pour into jelly bag or into a colander lined with several thicknesses of 100 percent cotton cheesecloth. Allow juice to drip out for several hours.

3. Squeeze grape pulp gently to get as much juice as possible, but without squeezing pulp through the bag. Measure 4⅔ cups juice; set aside. Into a small bowl, squeeze juice of lemon and orange. Set aside. Scrape out white membranes and discard. Slice peels into extremely thin slices. In a small saucepan, combine peels with 2 cups *water*. Bring to a boil. Lower heat and simmer for 3 minutes. Drain and reserve peels. Discard liquid.

4. In a 5- to 6-quart Dutch oven, combine the 4⅔ cups grape juice and the citrus juices. Add pectin and margarine. Bring to a rolling boil, stirring constantly. Add sugar, raisins, nuts, and peels. Return to a full, rolling boil. Boil hard 1 minute.

5. Remove from heat. Quickly skim off foam with a metal spoon. Ladle at once into hot, sterilized half-pint jars, leaving a ¼-inch headspace. Adjust lids. Process in boiling water bath canner for 15 minutes. Cool on wire rack, inverting jars occasionally to keep fruit and nuts distributed. Makes 9 to 10 half-pints.

Note: This may be made with juice concentrate mixed with water according to directions if grapes are unavailable.

Potato Latke

3	large baking potatoes (about 1½ pounds)
2	slightly beaten eggs
½	teaspoon salt
⅛	teaspoon pepper
¾	cup cooking oil
	Dairy sour cream, chives (optional)

1. Wash, peel, and finely shred potatoes. Place in a colander and rinse; squeeze by hand to drain liquid. In a large bowl, stir together potatoes, eggs, salt, and pepper.

2. In a 12-inch skillet, heat ½ cup of the oil over medium-high heat. Drop large spoonfuls (about ¼ cup) of potato mixture into hot oil; flatten to a thin cake (about 4 inches in diameter).

3. Cook cakes, 3 or 4 at a time, for 2 to 3 minutes on each side or until golden brown. Adjust heat and add the remaining ¼ cup oil as necessary during cooking. Drain on paper towels. Serve warm with sour cream and chives, if desired. Makes 12 latkes.

{ Comfort }

LET THE NORTH WIND HOWL. You'll be safe inside, enveloped by the warmth of country's

favorite winter touches. Surround yourself with cozy blankets, wool rugs,

and handmade throws in traditional country colors and fabrics. They'll help you ward off

the season's chill while adding comfort and style to your home.

Winter Warm-Ups

Savor the pleasures of the season: a pot of tea, a good book, and a crackling fire. 1. Nothing soothes like a nice cup of tea. To enjoy teas made from your own herbs, make individual bags by opening a purchased teabag and tracing it onto cheesecloth. Stitch the long edges together, then fold the bag and fill both sides with dried herbs. Fold the top edges down and staple them to the bag. Use tags from an office supply store to label the tea bags. **2.** Give your fireplace a cozy look by hanging vintage wool blankets above the mantel. Install a quilt rack or decorative drapery rod on the chimney breast, positioning it so the blankets fall to the mantel shelf or just below (but well away from the firebox so there's no danger of sparks coming in contact with them). For a fragrant fire, use fruit woods, such as apple, mulberry, or cherry, or add hickory or piñon logs. Or toss bundles of lavender, sage, or cinnamon sticks onto the fire once it's burning well.

Cozy up your bedroom with plump pillows and warm covers. **1.** For instant pillows, roll up wool blankets and knitted throws. Tie them with twine to hold them in a neckroll shape. **2.** Make your bed a cocoon with soft pillows and flannel sheets. If you love sleeping under heavy covers, layer blankets and quilts under a matelassé spread. If you prefer a light covering, opt for a down-filled duvet. Using fabric generously helps promote a feeling of warmth, so be sure to dress the bed with a skirt that can puddle on the floor. Or turn an oversize blanket into a bed skirt; drape it over your box spring and let it fall to the floor.

Blanket Statements

You don't have to confine blankets to the bed to create a feeling of cozy warmth. Try these ideas for working vintage or new coverlets and blankets into your decorating scheme: Lay a woven coverlet over the dining table or drape one over a tea table in the living room for touchable texture. Stitch curtain rings to the edge of a blanket, then hang the blanket from a rod to curtain off a room. Or hang blankets from a bed canopy to cut down drafts and create a snug sense of enclosure. Toss a blanket over a chair for a quick slipcover. Hang a vintage patterned blanket on the wall as you would a quilt, or throw it over a stair rail. Use scraps of worn cotton or wool blankets to stitch up pillows or to cover a footstool. Stack folded collectible blankets in an open cupboard or armoire and let their colors and textures enhance a room's feeling of warmth.

GOOD ★ NITE

2

«Soft colors, such as winter white, light gray, and ivory, all freshen a room while giving it the snowy palette of winter. To keep colors from seeming cold, warm them up with fabrics in cozy textures.»

Stitch up a cuddly fleece blanket and pillow for snuggling next to the fire. **1.** To make the blanket, use two fleece throws (about 50×60 inches), or purchase fleece by the yard at a fabric store and piece it to this size. Place the throws right sides together, then spread a layer of thin quilt batting on top. Machine-stitch through the three layers 1 inch from the edge, leaving a 12-inch opening for turning. Clip the corners on the diagonal and turn the blanket right side out. Stitch the opening closed. With a disappearing marking pen, draw a scroll design on the blanket. Stitch the design with embroidery floss, using ¾-inch-long stitches. Also make a double row of ¾-inch-long stitches 6 inches in from the edges. **2.** To make the pillow, use a purchased throw or fleece yardage. Cut one front piece 20×20 inches and two back pieces 20×13 inches. Hem one long edge of one back piece, then place the back pieces on the front piece, right sides facing and raw edges aligned; place the hemmed edge of the back piece under the unfinished edge of the remaining back piece (the hemmed edge will be on the outside when you turn the case right side out). Stitch ½ inch from the edges. Clip the corners and turn right side out. With embroidery floss, make a double row of ¾-inch-long stitches 1 inch in from the edges. Insert a pillow through the back flap.

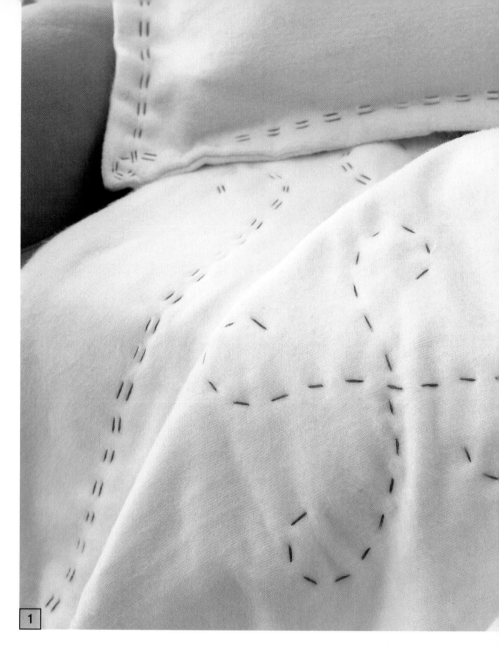

1

《 Warm your living room for winter with touchable textures and a rich layering of accessories. Create a mantel display with wood-framed prints and mirrors and assemble lanterns or candles for glowing light. 》

Fill your winter home with furnishings and accents inspired by nature. **1.** Fragrant pine sweeps have long been used to scent cupboards, closets, and drawers. To make your own, cut stems of white pine, which has long, soft needles. Bundle the stems and trim the ends so they're even. Starting at the bottom, wrap the stems tightly with seam binding or ribbon. When you reach the top of the stems, secure the end of the seam binding or ribbon with hot glue. Trim the handle with braid at the stem end and below the needles, hot-gluing the braid in place. Keep several pine sweeps around the house, and give them as holiday or post-Christmas gifts to brush away winter gloom. **2.** Use furnishings made from twigs, branches, and other natural materials to evoke a rustic lodge perched on a snowy peak. Look for pieces made by artisans in your area, then accent them with mission-style lamps, plus curtains and cushions made from soft flannels and cottons in bold colors and prints.

Camp It Up

Inspired by nature, camp-style decorating includes these elements.

- Choose Turkish rugs with vibrant vegetable-dye colors. These shades work well with wood interiors.
- Combine distressed leather with richly colored plaids or chenille.
- Accessorize with camp-style crafts—anything whittled, woven, or otherwise made by hand.

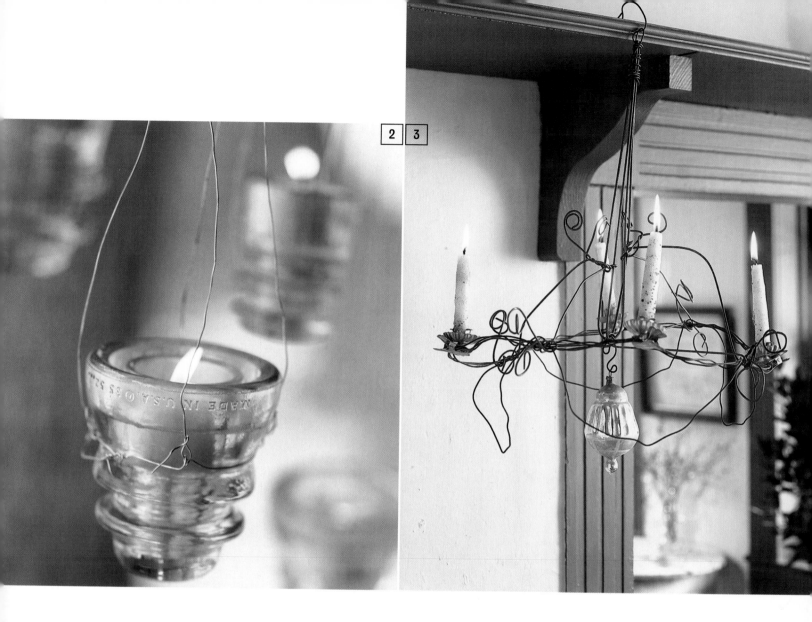

Winter Lights

Banish winter darkness with the warm glow of candlelight. 1. To make the bases of these candleholders, you'll need 3-inch-thick pieces of wood and 18-gauge tie wire from a hardware store. These wood pieces came from an old yellow-pine quilting frame, but you can use logs for a more rustic look. Using a drill bit the same size as the 18-gauge wire, drill a hole in each wood piece, off center. Glue one end of the wire into the hole; spiral the wire around a candle, shaping it as needed to hold the candle securely in place. **2.** Old telephone pole insulators make great votive candleholders. Look for them at flea markets; wrap with wire to make a cradle and hanger. **3.** For a free-form chandelier, wrap 18-gauge tie wire three or four times in a circle. Attach additional lengths of wire at four evenly spaced points around the circle; shape them as desired, adding spirals and curlicues. Bring four lengths together for a hanger. Attach candles using Christmas tree candle clips; hang an ornament from the bottom.

Experience the beauty of winter through outdoor country-style decorations and activities. **1.** For a soft winter glow after the holidays, use your Christmas lights on a bundle of branches. Collect a few stems of forsythia, yellow-twig dogwood, or another shrub from your yard; tie the stems tightly with heavy twine. Wrap a string of miniature Christmas lights through the branches as if you were decorating a tree upside down, then hang the bundle near a doorway. **2.** Celebrate a snow day with an outdoor picnic. Brush the snow off the picnic table and cover it with an old quilt or blanket, then spread out a portable feast. A camping stove quickly heats up a hearty chili or soup. Serve it in enamelware cups so there's no worry about breakage. Bring hot coffee and hot cocoa in thermoses, and pack an assortment of biscuits, chips, and breadsticks for quick energy.

The Great Outdoors

To enjoy the outdoors during the winter months, try these ideas.

- Make luminarias by filling clay pots with sand and gravel, then placing hurricane shades and candles on top.
- Furnish your yard with winterproof seating and garden ornaments.
- Plant flowers and herbs that, when dried, will attract wildlife during the cold months. Good choices include sunflowers, wild rose hips, and globe amaranth.

《 **Snowy winter months** create a hushed beauty even on the coldest days. To make the most of your outdoor space, be sure to include seating, lighting, decorations, and snacks for wildlife.

2

{ Remember }

FAMILY HISTORY LONG HAS BEEN PRESERVED through scrapbooks, photo albums, and personal journals. Continue the tradition by taking advantage of cold winter days to organize mementos for generations to come. Scapbooks and albums work just fine, but here are a few creative ideas for keeping and displaying treasured snapshots and memorabilia.

1

Faces & Places

Try these creative ideas for keeping family photos and heirlooms on display where you can enjoy them every day. **1.** If you're lucky enough to have family tintypes, hang them in a swag across a doorway. To make a cradle for each tintype, bend 18-gauge wire into a horseshoe shape; then bend the wire ends up to hold the tintype (like an easel), crimping them snugly. Attach the holders to a length of chain from a hardware store; use three links of chain to secure each image to the longer chain. Space the pictures evenly, and hang the swag from small nails tapped into the door frame. **2.** For a bulletin board that requires no tacks, make a memory grid from a window frame and twine. Find an old frame at a flea market or salvage shop. Hammer tacks into the back of the frame along the sides, then wrap heavy twine around the tacks. Crisscross them on the front, stretching the twine so it's taut. At the points where the twine crosses on the front, secure it with a small brad. Tuck your favorite photos and postcards between the strings.

Add to the character of old photos by using vintage materials in their display. **1.** Shop antiques stores for an old tea tray with a glass insert, or find an old frame and have a piece of glass cut to fit. (Attach drawer-pull-style handles to the sides; paint them to match.) At a copy center, enlarge a photo to the required size; position it behind the glass and add a cardboard backing. **2.** To display tintypes or photos bellpull-style, attach them to wide ribbon with double-stick carpet tape. Nail the ribbon to the door; hang an old pocketwatch or other keepsake over the nail.

Preserving Family Memories

Good storage is the key to keeping family memorabilia intact. Visit local art supply stores and crafts shops to find containers that suit your needs. Mailing tubes hold children's artwork. Labeled cardboard boxes store everything from a summer vacation videotape collection to computer disks with images from a digital camera. Label your containers clearly so future generations will be able to identify the contents and appreciate their value.

Photographs of family and friends are constant reminders of love and support in your life. Keep them close at hand on desks and tabletops. **1.** For a photo gallery that's also a practical desk accessory, start with two glass cylinders or vases, one slightly smaller in diameter than the other (look for these at crafts shops or florist's supply stores, or check gift shops for glass vases in a variety of heights and diameters). Place the smaller container inside the larger one, then slide photos into the space between the vases. Use the container for paintbrushes or a bouquet of flowers. **2.** Black-and-white or sepia-tone photography has a classic look that's at home in a country-style room. To give even new photos this vintage character, photocopy color photos on a color copier set to black. For a sepia tone, use only the brown color setting. Choose frames that enhance the photos without overwhelming them. Display them with a mix of treasures passed down from family and friends.

{ Anticipation }

WINTER HAS ITS CHARMS, but who can resist the color and fragrance of fresh,

blooming flowers indoors? Preview spring with forced bulbs and branches

and a miniature plot of lawn in a tray or tureen. The natural perfumes and bright hues will

bridge those late winter months before early spring blooms.

Bulbs

Get a glimpse of spring through the beauty of easy-to-force bulbs.
1. Paperwhite narcissus respond readily to light and water and have become a favorite for Christmas gifts. They're among the easiest bulbs to force because they don't need the 12 to 15 weeks of cold storage that most bulbs require (just give them two weeks in a cool, dark spot). You don't even need to plant them in soil—simply perch the bulbs on vintage milk bottles filled with water, and enjoy the beauty of roots reaching down and stems stretching up. Keep the water level just below the base of the bulbs to avoid the danger of rotting. **2.** To force hyacinths, purchase pre-cooled bulbs from a nursery or mail-order catalog. You can grow them in water or set them in soil. Keep them in a cool, dark location until shoots emerge, then move them to successively brighter spots in the house over a period of several days. Keep the soil evenly moist and add decorative gravel around the bulbs, if you like. Hyacinths require six to eight weeks to grow 2 to 3 inches tall.

2

Fresh greenery and budding branches bring a breath of spring indoors.

1. Paperwhite narcissus bulbs are easy to force, and their bright green stems and aromatic flowers are welcome reminders that spring is on its way. Starting even before the holidays, begin forcing bulbs every two weeks or so for a constant supply of blossoms through the winter months. Line up several along a sunny windowsill to frame your view; vintage goblets or specialized containers can accommodate one bulb each for a striking display. Narcissus blooms will last about a week or two if kept in a cool room. The plants are too tender to survive outdoors in most regions, so just discard the bulbs when the flowers fade. You also can satisfy your craving for green and growing things with houseplants and a small patch of lawn growing in a washtub or other container. **2.** In anticipation of spring, you can force branches of spring-blooming trees and shrubs into early bloom. From the time you cut the branches until they bloom, several weeks will pass, allowing you to enjoy the twiggy stems throughout the final weeks of winter. For complete instructions on cutting and forcing branches, see page 200.

Growing Grass Indoors

For a stand of grass that doesn't need mowing, follow these tips.

- Spread a layer of pebbles in the bottom of a container for drainage, then fill the container with good potting soil mixed with peat. Water the soil.
- Sow wheatberries or annual grass, such as rye, over the soil. Pat seeds lightly to make sure they're in touch with the soil. Place in a sunny spot.
- Sprinkle or mist soil when it starts to dry out, keeping it evenly moist.

Branches

Forcing branches brings flowering shrubs and trees into bloom for late-winter enjoyment. 1. Arrange branches for forcing in the vase you want to display them in, or keep them in buckets until they begin blooming. **2.** Use sharp, clean pruning shears to cut the branch flush with the main branch. Keep in mind that you're pruning the shrub or tree with these cuts, so choose branches whose removal will enhance the shape and growth of the plant. Using a sharp knife, scrape a few inches of bark off the cut end, then make a 2-inch-deep vertical slit in the stem end with the pruning shears. This will help the stem absorb more water. **3.** Place the branches in a vase or bucket filled with room-temperature water and set the vase in a brightly lit spot (but not in direct sunlight). Add fresh water to the vase as needed. To increase humidity around the buds, tie a plastic drycleaner's bag over the branches and vase; remove it when the buds swell. **4.** After several weeks, the buds will open into full flower, ahead of the natural cycle outdoors.

Branches for Winter Forcing

Good candidates for winter forcing include flowering quince, star magnolia, forsythia, pussy willow, witch hazel, redbud, and fruit trees. You'll need to cut the branches at least five weeks before their normal flowering time, when the buds are just beginning to swell (you can distinguish them from the leaf buds because they're a little fatter).

1

2
3 4

Spring Clutter Buster

1. Vintage garden accessories make wonderful accents indoors or out. For spring, use the urn to help you get organized—it's perfect for holding magazines you haven't read yet or back issues you want to keep for future reference.

1 2

Summer Wine Cooler

2. Fill the urn with ice and chill your favorite summer wines and champagnes in casual country style. Of course, it works just as well for sodas, lemonade, tea, or bottled waters. Place it on the porch or patio for outdoor parties and barbecues. Indoors, it's a portable bar; stand it on a barrel or countertop where glasses will be handy. Just be sure to protect the surrounding surface from any moisture that might drip when you remove chilled bottles to pour.

Autumn Bread Basket

3. For an after-football party with a menu of build-your-own sandwiches, fill the urn with crusty loaves of bread. Spread a tea towel over the mouth of the urn, then arrange the breads. Have a bread board and knife nearby so guests can cut slices of their favorites.

3 | 4

Holiday Decorating

4. To make your urn a holiday focal point, place a large pillar candle in the center and fill in around it with mixed nuts. If the urn is quite deep, place a terra-cotta pot upside down inside it to raise the candle to the desired height. Fill in around the pot with crumpled newspaper or recycled packing peanuts to within an inch of the rim. Then fill in with mixed nuts in the shell. Add a few apples and sprigs of pine around the base for color and holiday fragrance.

Spring Wreath

Buy a square grapevine frame from a crafts store. Or weave your own by turning a four-legged stool upside down and using the legs as a frame for wrapping the vines. (The best time to make grapevine wreaths is fall, when the vines are mature but flexible.) Glue on pads of moss, using a hot-glue gun. Empty 2½ dozen eggs, using the method on page 23, and glue them in place.

Summer Wreath

Wrap a 9-inch-diameter plastic-foam wreath form with wide white satin ribbon, gluing the ends to the back of the wreath. Tie twine around the top of the wreath for a hanger. Sort shells by size, and use 5-minute epoxy (from a hardware store or a crafts store) to glue the largest ones to the face of the wreath. After the epoxy has set, attach medium-size and small shells over the large ones. Add smaller shells to the inside and outside edges to round out the shape and cover the ribbon.

Autumn Wreath

Start with a purchased or homemade grapevine wreath and an assortment of items collected on walks in the woods—milkweed pods, sweetgum or sycamore balls, acorns, leaves, and pinecones work well. Using a hot-glue gun, affix pads of sheet moss or sphagnum moss over three evenly spaced sections of the wreath. Then glue the pods and other natural materials to the moss and the vines. Lightly spritz the entire wreath with copper or bronze spray paint. Loosely and randomly wrap the wreath with lengths of galvanized wreath wire, twisting the wire ends into curlicues.

Winter Wreath

For the wreath form, use a 9x12- or 11x14-inch picture frame (crafts stores carry unfinished frames with wide, flat moldings designed for decorating with dried materials). Cover the frame with sphagnum moss, using hot glue or spool wire to secure the moss. Collect berried branches, such as winterberry or possum haw, and cut the branches into pieces slightly shorter than the sides of the frame. Wire several pieces together at the cut ends, then wire the bundle to the frame. Repeat to cover all four sides, then glue in additional berried twigs to fill out the frame and hide all cut ends.

SPRING

18-19: **Latex paints on eggs:** 1745 Lemon Whip, 1746 Ornate Yellow, 1610 Sea Nymph, 1660 Sea Oat, 1635 Catawba Grape from Pratt & Lambert, available at paint and hardware stores. **Myrtle topiary:** Gateway Gardens, 800/890-0655.

22: **Latex paints on eggs:** 2693 Blueberry Frost, 2694 Violeta, 2695 Tint of Lilac, 2098 Alaskan Morn, 2099 Blue Fox Frost, Pittsburgh Paint, available at paint and hardware stores.

24: **Pegboard** #K203, Shaker Workshops, 800/840-9121.

25: **Desk, chair, accessories:** The Comfort Common, 717 High St., Comfort, TX 78301; 830/995-3030.

26: **Peg rack:** Barbara Trujillo Antiques, 2466 Main St., Bridgehampton, NY 11932; 631/537-3838. **Towels:** The Ralph Lauren Home Collection, 212/642-8700. **Fish rug:** #11052 Celestial Shells, 4x6 feet, The Rug Market, 800/422-4354.

27: **Wooden hooks, top right:** #HK-W from Harbor Farm, 800/342-8003; finished with Muylands Wax, 888/369-5263.

31: **Linen toweling:** Kidron Town & Country Store, see under Pages 48–51.

34-35: **Kitchen designer:** Megan Whitehouse, ASID, CKD, Whitehouse Design Inc., 603/644-8484. **Flooring:** Southern Pine Council, 504/443-4464; www.southernpine.com. **Cabinetry:** Akurum with Land solid beaded-board doors from IKEA, 800/434-4532. **Paint:** #F29 Seagrass, #E11 Cornmeal, Martha Stewart Everyday Colors, Kmart. **Platters, dishes, yellowware:** Faye Foster Antiques and Interiors, 4 Central Square, Bristol, NH 03222; 603/744-9130. **Pendant light,** similar available: #19771, pewter hanging light, The Renovator's Supply, 800/659-0203, Dept. 2442. **Windsor chairs, table:** D.R. Dimes and Co., 603/942-7409.

36-37: **Lab stool and fabric at windows** (windowpane sheer white): from Room No. 5, 237-½ E. Main St., Fredericksburg, TX 78624; 830/997-1090. Similar **chandelier** available from Homestead, 223 E. Main St., Fredericksburg, TX 78624; 830/997-5551.

39: **Tea towel for curtain:** Sur La Table, 800/243-0852. **Iron table:** Bountiful, 1335 Abbot Kinney Rd., Venice, CA 90291; 310/450-3620.

40: **Antiques and collectibles** from Old Lucketts Store, 42350 Lucketts Rd., Leesburg, VA 20176; 703/779-0268. For interior design consultation, contact Amy Krogh at that number.

41: **Enamel letters** similar to those shown available from Homestead, see under Pages 36–37. **Porcelain doll pitcher** from American Higgledy Piggledy, 417 E. Main St., Fredericksburg, TX 78624; 830/997-5551.

42-43: **Framed wallpaper:** #RDW-310 Renaissance Damask, #GLW-935 Glenwood, #BRW-935 Briar Rose from Bradbury & Bradbury Art Wallpapers, 707/746-1900; www.bradbury.com. **Frames:** #316280-155 Document Frame 11x14 inch, in walnut, black, gray, or natural from Umbra, Inc., 800/387-5122. **Table, chair:** from Vance Kitira International; for the nearest store, call 800/646-6360. **Skirt, curtain fabric:** #8187 Cordia from Zimmer-Rohde, to the trade only; 212/627-8080. **Tieback ribbon:** #4651 Tubular Organdy #31

pink from Mokuba Ribbon, available through JKM Products, 856/767-6604; www.festivegiftwrap.com. **Conservatory ledge:** #LE36, 36-inch, white from French Wyres, P.O. Box 131655, Tyler, TX 75713; 903/561-1742. **Pots:** #GP6 Garden Pot, 6-inch; #GP4 Garden Pot 4-inch, mushroom; #ER6 European Rose Pot, 6-inch, white crackle; #PP6 Piazza Pot, 6-inch; #VP4 Villa Pot, 5-inch, butter; all with matching saucers extra; from Potluck Studios, 23 Main St., Accord, NY 12404; 914-626-2300. **Paint:** walls, Cornhusk; back of bookshelves, Wild Rose, Martha Stewart Everyday Colors, at Kmart.

44-46: **Antique and reproduction furnishings:** America. Antiques & Emporium. Interior design concepts, America.Home Division. Contact both at 26 S. Third St., Newark, OH 43055; 740/345-0588.

47: **Sink skirt fabric,** #595918 Falmouth Check, cowslip, $20/yard, Laura Ashley. **Wall paint,** #HC-4 Hawthorne Yellow, Benjamin Moore & Co.

48-51: **Cabinetry and shelving:** Plain & Fancy Custom Cabinetry; **countertop, sink, window sills:** Avonite Solid Surfacing; **faucet:** Kohler; **table:** Drexel Heritage; **fabric:** Arte and Summer Hill. **Linen dish toweling** 100 percent linen, 18 inches wide, available by the yard ($6.98) from Kidron Town & Country Store, 4959 Kidron Rd., Kidron, OH 44636; fax 330/857-3023; or visit the website at www.kidrontc.com. Order number K510 and state border color: red, green, blue, or yellow.

52: Look for **vintage aprons** at flea markets and antiques shops and malls. Or check with Lottie Ballou, 130 W. E St., Benicia, CA 94510; 707/747-9433; or call Bagley Home, P.O. Box 1984, Sag Harbor, NY 11963; 631/725-3553.

54-55: **Cabinet:** Antiques at Mayfair, 119 Rt. 101A, Amherst, NH 03031; 603/595-7531.

56-57: **Interior designers:** Jim Lord and Bobby Dent, 717 High St., Comfort, TX 78013; 830/995-3030. **Floor lamp, coffee table, end table, splay-leg table, pillows** from The Comfort Common, same address and phone. **Pillow fabric:** floral, Helena, natural; check, Turner, sage; Calico Corners, 800/213-6366. **Armoire, sisal rug:** The Homestead, 223 E. Main, Fredericksburg, TX 78624; 830/997-5551. **Wall paint:** #3W23-3 Washed Khaki; trim, #3W23-1 Mountain Top; Devoe Paint. For nearest dealer, call 888/681-6353; www.devoepaint.com.

SUMMER

62-66: **Seashells:** Contact The Shell Warehouse, Mallory Square, 1 Whitehead St., Key West, FL 33040; 305/294-5168; or call U.S. Shell, Inc., 956/943-1709, for their nearest store. **Aqua cupboard,** Wendy W. Blackey, Grindstone Farm Antiques, Webster, NH; 603/746-5924.

74, 78: Visit The Gamble Flower Farm at 9000 Carmel Valley Rd., Carmel, CA 93923; call 831/626-9141 for hours. Cut your own flowers from the cutting garden; rose plants also available. For seeds or transplants of the annuals and perennials in Susanna Gamble's arrangements, check local nurseries; for mail-order sources, call Thompson & Morgan Inc., 800/274-7333, or White Flower Farm, 800/503-9624, for a catalog.

79: **Interior design** by Roberta Brown Root, design consultant, Seattle, WA; 206/522-5112. **Blue bench,** Randy L. Hoehn, available at Miller Pollard

Interiors, 2575 NE University Village, Seattle, WA 98105; 206/527-8478.

80-82: See under pages 74 and 78.

88-89: If you're interested in collecting **antique wicker picnicware,** one source is Mary Jean McLaughlin, 105 Old Lyme St., Box 466, Old Lyme, CT 06731; 860/434-1896. For **20th-century mixing bowls, condiment jars, and Bakelite utensils,** contact Penny and Peter Jones at Penny Toys, P.O. Box 302, Leola, PA 17540; 717/656-0678; www.pennytoys.com. For **enamelware,** contact David Pikul, The Chuctanunda Antique Company, 1 Fourth Ave., Amsterdam, NY 12010; 518/843-3983; www.enameledwareed.com; or e-mail dpikul@telenet.net. For **1930s–1950s luncheon tablecloths,** contact antiques dealer Nancy Reece, P.O. Box 551, Adamstown, PA 19501; or call 717/336-2177 on Sundays. Look for **old fruit jars and glass jars** at flea markets and antiques shows, or search eBay at www.ebay.com.

94: **Architect:** Kathrine F. McCoy, AIA; **wicker sofa and chair, sign:** Ted Meyer's Harbor Antiques, Montauk Hwy, Wainscott, NY 11975-0043.

95: **Fresco, pillows, coverlet:** from Paula Hamilton by hand, 520/623-5343.

96–97: **Design:** Mark McCormick Art & Antiques, 8837 Schmalz, St. Jacob, IL 62281; 618/667-7789.

AUTUMN

104: **Dinner plate:** #4203010 Cucina Fresca, saffron, 10½ inch; Dining and Co., 800/220-4871.

106: **Copper tape:** Detailed Stained Glass, 51 S. Main St., Concord, NH 03301; 603/224-7100.

107: **Yellowware:** Concord Antique Gallery, 97 Storrs St., Concord, NH 03301; 603/225-2070.

108-11: **Acorns and pinecones:** from Land of Sky Nurseries, 108 Lakewood Dr., Asheville, NC 28803; 828/252-5962. **Folding screen** from Welch's Way Farm, 1377 Battle St., Webster NH 03303; 603/648-2372. **Lamp:** custom made by A. Jay's Accessories, 27B Jackson St., Concord, NH 03301; 603/225-9926; e-mail: ajaysacc@aol.com. **Bed** from Welch's Way Farm, see above. **Coverlet, sheets, bedskirt,** Garnet Hill; call 800/622-6216 for a catalog. **Blanket,** Laura Fisher/Antique Quilts and Americana, 1050 Second Ave., Gallery #84, New York, NY 10022; 212/838-2596.

112: **Chairs, sofa, mirror, candleholders, large clock, side table** from English Country Antiques, Nake Hollow Rd., Bridgehampton, NY 11932; 631/537-0606.

115: **Salt-glaze jar** from Colonial Williamsburg, Prentis Store, P.O. Box 1776, Williamsburg, VA 23187-1776; 800/446-9240.

118: **Gourds, pepperberries, pods:** check your local crafts store. Or call Knud Neilsen Co. to find the nearest dealer, 800/698-5656.

119: You can order **pressed leaves** from Nature's Press, 800/850-2499. **Bread trough:** The Seraph, 531 Main St., Sturbridge, MA 01518; 508/347-2241.

120-21: Visit Apple Hill Farm, 580 Mountain Road, (NH Rt. 132), Concord, NH 03301 mid-June through Thanksgiving. Call 603/224-8862 for hours. To find pick-your-own apple orchards in your area, check the Yellow Pages or call the local chamber of commerce.

132-37: **Alphabet cookie cutters,** #3618 Mack Cutters Alphabet, $20 (includes shipping); #3619 Mack Cutters Numbers, $12 (includes shipping); Kitchen Arts, 161 Newbury St., Boston, MA 02116; 617/266-8701.

WINTER

144: **Antique and reproduction furnishings:** see under Pages 44–46. **Apple cone** (on newel post) from Colonial Williamsburg; for a catalog, call 800/446-9240.

152-53, 157: **Antique and reproduction furnishings:** America. Antiques & Emporium. Interior design concepts, America.Home Division. See under Pages 44–46.

158: **Feather-shape cookie cutters,** 9-inch $18.95, 7-inch $13.95 from The Victor Trading Co., 719/689-2346; www.victortradingco.com. **Vintage McCoy pots** (left photo) and **similar tree stands** with 2-inch-diameter cup for tree trunk available from Hikchik, 417 Maple, West Des Moines, IA; 515/255-0588; www.hikchik.com.

160: **Ironstone covered vegetable dish** from Faye Foster Antiques and Interiors, 4 Central Square, Bristol, NH 03222; 603/744-9130.

161: **Chair upholstery fabric** is a tablecloth from Parkside Gallery, 17–19 W. Main St., Hillsboro, NH 03244; 603/464-3322.

162: **Yellowware bowls,** Parkside Gallery, 17-19 W. Main St., Hillsboro, NH 03244; 603/464-3322.

174-75: **Iron moose menorah** available from The Store at Sugarbush, Route 100, Waitsfield, VT; 802/496-4465 or 800/639-8031; order on-line at www.vermontstore.com. Menorah measures 15½x15 inches, $80. **Blue-striped plates,** Target.

180: **Rolled fringed blanket** as pillow is wool camel and cream throw, 60x72 inches, by Melin Tregwint from Paulette Rollo. For the nearest store, call 207/563-5310. **Knitted rolled pillow** is Lakeland Cotton Throw, natural, 50x60 inches, Faribault Woolen Mill Co. **Striped spread** is vintage blanket from Cloud Works, 120 Tyler Rd., Contoocook, NH 03229; 603/746-6396.

181: **"Good Nite" sign** from The Comfort Common, see under Page 25. **Iron bed,** The Homestead; see under Pages 56–57.

185: **Twig mosaic book case** by artist Peter Winter. **Interior design, most furnishings and accessories** by Moose Creek, Ltd., 1592 Central Ave., Albany, NY 12205; 518/869-0049; or 10 State Rt. 10, Lake George, NY 12845; 518/745-7340; www.moosecreekltd.com.

191: **Vintage and flea market finds,** Hikchik, 417 Maple St., West Des Moines, IA 50265; 515/255-0588.

196-97: For mail-order sources of **amaryllis, hyacinth,** and **paperwhite bulbs,** contact the following: John Scheepers, Inc. 860/567-0838; White Flower Farm, 800/255-2852; www.800allbulb.com; Burpee Seed Co., 800/888-1447; Park Seed, 800/845-3369; Smith & Hawken, 800/776-3336.

198: **Glider, chair** from Zonal Home Interiors, 2139 Polk St., San Francisco, CA 94109; 415/563-2220. www.zonalhome.com.

{ Credits }

SPRING

8: produced by **MARY ANNE THOMSON**; photo, **KING AU/STUDIO AU**

9: wreath design, **JAMES CRAMER** and **DEAN JOHNSON**; photo, **TOM MCWILLIAM**

10–17: produced by **MATTHEW MEAD**; photos, **MONICA BUCK**

18–22: produced by **MATTHEW MEAD**; photos, **MONICA BUCK**

23: produced by **MEREDITH LADIK**; photo, **KING AU/STUDIO AU**

24: produced by **MEREDITH LADIK**; photos, **KING AU/STUDIO AU**

25: interior design by **JIM LORD** and **BOBBY DENT**; produced by **HELEN THOMPSON**; photo, **KING AU/STUDIO AU**

26: produced by **MARY EMMERLING**; photo, **WILLIAM STITES**

27: top left, produced by **JAMES CRAMER** and **DEAN JOHNSON**; photo, **REED DAVIS**; bottom left, produced by **JAMES CRAMER** and **DEAN JOHNSON**; photo, **TOM MCWILLIAM**; top right, bottom right, produced by **MEREDITH LADIK**; photos, **KING AU/STUDIO AU**

28: left, produced by **JEAN NORMAN** and **MEREDITH LADIK**; photo, **KING AU/STUDIO AU**; center, design, **CAROL BOLTON**; photo, **JENNIFER JORDAN**; right, design, **AMY KROGH**; photo, **KING AU/STUDIO AU**

29: produced by **HELEN THOMPSON**; photo, **KING AU/STUDIO AU**

30–31: produced by **JEAN NORMAN** and **MEREDITH LADIK**; photos, **KING AU/STUDIO AU**

32–33: produced by **MATTHEW MEAD**; photos, **HELEN NORMAN**

34–35: interior design, **MATTHEW MEAD**; kitchen design, **MEGAN WHITEHOUSE / WHITEHOUSE DESIGN**; produced by **MEREDITH LADIK**; photo, **BILL HOLT**

36–37: interior design, **CAROL BOLTON**; produced by **NANCY E. INGRAM**; photos, **JENNIFER JORDAN**

38–39: top left, produced by **MATTHEW MEAD**; photos, **REED DAVIS**

39: top and bottom right, design, **LAUREL LOUDERBACH** of Laurels, St. Helena, California; photos, **JAMIE HADLEY**

40: interior design, **AMY KROGH**; photos, **KING AU/STUDIO AU**

41: left, interior design, **CAROL BOLTON**; produced by **NANCY E. INGRAM**, photo **JENNIFER JORDAN**; right, produced by **MATTHEW MEAD**; photo, **MONICA BUCK**

42–43: produced by **MEREDITH LADIK**; photos, **KING AU/STUDIO AU**

44–45: design, **CARL OLIVERIO**; produced by **JOETTA MOULDEN**; photo, **BRAD SIMMONS**

46: design, **CARL OLIVERIO**; produced by **JOETTA MOULDEN**; photo, **BRAD SIMMONS**

47: interior design by **TRICIA FOLEY**; photos, **KING AU/STUDIO AU**

48–51: kitchen sink skirt produced by **MEREDITH LADIK** and **DEB FELTON**; photo, **KING AU/STUDIO AU**; chair slipcover and tablecloth: designs **PAULA HAMILTON**; styling, **PEGGY JOHNSTON**; photo, **PETER KRUMHARDT**

52: produced by **JAMES CRAMER** and **DEAN JOHNSON**; photo, **TOM MCWILLIAM**

53: produced by **JAMES CRAMER** and **DEAN JOHNSON**; photos, **WILLIAM STITES**

54–55: produced by **MATTHEW MEAD**; photos, **JEFF MCNAMARA**

56–57: interior design by **JIM LORD** and **BOBBY DENT**; produced by **HELEN THOMPSON**; photo, **KING AU/STUDIO AU**

58–59: produced by **MATTHEW MEAD**; photos, **KING AU/STUDIO AU**

SUMMER

60–61: produced by **MATTHEW MEAD**; photos, **KING AU/STUDIO AU**

62–67: produced by **MATTHEW MEAD**; photos, **ALISON MIKSCH**

68: design, **MEREDITH LADIK**; photo, **WILLIAM STITES**

69–72: produced by **JAMES CRAMER** and **DEAN JOHNSON**; photos, **TOM MCWILLIAM**

73: produced by **MATTHEW MEAD**; photos, **ALISON MIKSCH**

74: flowers by **SUSANNA GAMBLE**; produced by **LINDA JOAN SMITH**; photo, **BILL HOLT**

75: photo, **WILLIAM STITES**

76: produced by **JAMES CRAMER** and **DEAN JOHNSON**; photo, **GARY GRAVES**

77: produced by **MEREDITH LADIK**; photo, **WILLIAM STITES**

78: flowers by **SUSANNA GAMBLE**; produced by **LINDA JOAN SMITH**; photo, **BILL HOLT**

79: interior design, **ROBERTA BROWN ROOT**; produced by **TRISH MAHARAM** and **BONNIE MAHARAM**; photo, **BILL HOLT**

80: flowers by **SUSANNA GAMBLE**; produced by **LINDA JOAN SMITH**; photo, **BILL HOLT**

81: produced by **MEREDITH LADIK**; photo, **WILLIAM STITES**

82–83: flowers by **SUSANNA GAMBLE**; produced by **LINDA JOAN SMITH**; photo, **BILL HOLT**

84–85: produced by **MATTHEW MEAD**; photos, **TOM MCWILLIAM**

86: produced by **MATTHEW MEAD**; left photo, **JIM KRANTZ**; right photo, **ALISON MIKSCH**

87: produced by **MATTHEW MEAD**; photo, **ALISON MIKSCH**

88–89: produced by **MATTHEW MEAD**; photos, **JIM KRANTZ**

90–91: produced by **MATTHEW MEAD**; photos, **MONICA BUCK**

92: left, design, **KATHY BARBOUR**; photo, **MICHAEL SKOTT**; right, created by **REBECCA COLE**; photo, **HELEN NORMAN**

93: photo, **ERIC ROTH**

94–95: designer, **MARK MCCORMICK**; produced by **MARY ANNE THOMSON**; photo, **KING AU/STUDIO AU**

96: produced by **MARY EMMERLING**; photo, **WILLIAM STITES**

97: design, **PAULA HAMILTON**; produced by **CLAUDIA FRANKLIN** and **MARY MULCAHY**; photo, **KING AU/STUDIO AU**

98–99: produced by **MATTHEW MEAD**; photos, **KING AU/STUDIO AU**

AUTUMN

100: produced by **MATTHEW MEAD**; photos, **REED DAVIS**

101: produced by **JAMES CRAMER** and **DEAN JOHNSON**; photo, **TOM MCWILLIAM**

102: produced by **MATTHEW MEAD**; photo, **MONICA BUCK**

103: produced by **JAMES CRAMER** and **DEAN JOHNSON**; photo, **TOM MCWILLIAM**

104–11: produced by **MATTHEW MEAD**; photos, **MONICA BUCK**

112–13: photo, **MICHAEL SKOTT**

114–15:	photo on 114 and 115 right, LYNE NEYMEYER; 114 left, TOM MCWILLIAM
116:	produced by JAMES CRAMER and DEAN JOHNSON; photo: WILLIAM STITES
117:	produced by JAMES CRAMER and DEAN JOHNSON; photo, GARY GRAVES
118–19:	produced by MATTHEW MEAD; photos, MONICA BUCK
120–21:	produced by MATTHEW MEAD; photos, REED DAVIS
122–23:	produced by MATTHEW MEAD; photos, JEFF MCNAMARA
124:	produced by MARY ANNE THOMSON; photo, BRYAN WHITNEY
125–31:	produced by MATTHEW MEAD; photos, LORIN M. GROSS
132–37:	produced by MATTHEW MEAD; photos, HELEN NORMAN
138–39:	produced by MATTHEW MEAD; photos, KING AU/STUDIO AU

WINTER

140–41:	produced by MATTHEW MEAD; photo, HELEN NORMAN
142–43:	produced by JAMES CRAMER and DEAN JOHNSON; photos, TOM MCWILLIAM
144:	decorations, CARL and RANDY OLIVERIO; produced by JOETTA MOULDEN; photo, BRAD SIMMONS
145:	left, produced by MATTHEW MEAD; photo, JIM KRANTZ; right, produced by MATTHEW MEAD; photo, REED DAVIS
146:	produced by MATTHEW MEAD; photo, REED DAVIS
147:	left, design, SUSAN BOARDMAN; produced by ESTELLE BOND GURALNICK; photo, ERIC ROTH; right, produced by MATTHEW MEAD; photo, REED DAVIS
148–49:	produced by MATTHEW MEAD; photo, MONICA BUCK
150:	produced by MATTHEW MEAD; photo, ERIC ROTH
151:	produced by MATTHEW MEAD; photo, REED DAVIS
152–53:	decorations, CARL and RANDY OLIVERIO; produced by JOETTA MOULDEN; photo, BRAD SIMMONS
154–56:	produced by JAMES CRAMER and DEAN JOHNSON; photos, MONICA BUCK
157:	left, produced by JAMES CRAMER and DEAN JOHNSON; photo, MONICA BUCK; right, design, CARL OLIVERIO; produced by JOETTA MOULDEN; photo, BRAD SIMMONS
158:	left, produced by JAMES CRAMER and DEAN JOHNSON; photo, KING AU/STUDIO AU; right, produced by MATTHEW MEAD; photo, REED DAVIS
159:	produced by JAMES CRAMER and DEAN JOHNSON; photo, WILLIAM STITES
160:	produced by MATTHEW MEAD; left photo, KING AU/STUDIO AU; right photo, JIM KRANTZ
161:	produced by MATTHEW MEAD; photo, JIM KRANTZ
162:	produced by MATTHEW MEAD; photo, REED DAVIS
163:	produced by MATTHEW MEAD; photo top left, REED DAVIS; photos top and bottom right, KING AU/STUDIO AU
164–65:	produced by MATTHEW MEAD; photos, MONICA BUCK
166–67:	produced by MATTHEW MEAD; photos, ALISON MIKSCH
168–69:	produced by KATHRYN PRECOURT; photo, MONICA BUCK
170:	left, produced by KATHRYN PRECOURT; photo, MONICA BUCK; right, produced by JAMES CRAMER and DEAN JOHNSON; photo, JEFF MCNAMARA

171:	decorations, CARL and RANDY OLIVERIO; produced by JOETTA MOULDEN; photo, BRAD SIMMONS
172–73:	produced by MATTHEW MEAD; photos, MONICA BUCK
174–75:	produced by PEGGY JOHNSTON; photo, KING AU/STUDIO AU
176–77:	food stylist, DIANNA NOLIN; photos, ANDY LYONS
178:	produced by MATTHEW MEAD; photo, ALISON MIKSCH
179:	produced by JAMES CRAMER and DEAN JOHNSON, photo WILLIAM STITES
180:	produced by MATTHEW MEAD; photo, MONICA BUCK
181:	interior design by JIM LORD and BOBBY DENT; produced by HELEN THOMPSON; photo, KING AU/STUDIO AU
182–83:	design, PAULA HAMILTON; styling, PEGGY JOHNSTON; photos, PETER KRUMHARDT
184:	produced by MATTHEW MEAD; photo, KING AU/STUDIO AU
185:	interior design, STEVE MOMROW, Moose Creek Limited; photo, KING AU/STUDIO AU
186–88:	produced by JAMES CRAMER and DEAN JOHNSON; photos, TOM MCWILLIAM
189:	produced by MATTHEW MEAD; photo, HELEN NORMAN
190:	produced by JAMES CRAMER and DEAN JOHNSON; photo, TOM MCWILLIAM
191:	design, SHELLEY CALDWELL; photo, KING AU/STUDIO AU
192–93:	produced by JAMES CRAMER and DEAN JOHNSON; photos, TOM MCWILLIAM
194:	produced by MATTHEW MEAD; photo, HELEN NORMAN
195:	photo, MICHAEL SKOTT
196:	produced by JAMES CRAMER and DEAN JOHNSON; photo, TOM MCWILLIAM
197:	produced by JAMES CRAMER and DEAN JOHNSON; photo, MONICA BUCK
198:	produced by TIRZAH WANLASS; photo, JAMIE HADLEY
199:	produced by JAMES CRAMER and DEAN JOHNSON; photo, REED DAVIS
200–201:	produced by BONNIE MAHARAM; photos, BILL HOLT
202–203:	produced by MATTHEW MEAD; photos, KING AU/STUDIO AU
204:	photo, left, by REED DAVIS; photo, right, by JIM KRANTZ
205:	produced by JAMES CRAMER and DEAN JOHNSON; photo, TOM MCWILLIAM
206:	left, produced by JAMES CRAMER and DEAN JOHNSON; photo, TOM MCWILLIAM; right, produced by MATTHEW MEAD; photo, KING AU/STUDIO AU
207:	left, produced by JAMES CRAMER and DEAN JOHNSON; photo, TOM MCWILLIAM; right, produced by MATTHEW MEAD; photo, HELEN NORMAN

If you love country style, you'll find more great decorating ideas in these titles from Meredith Books.

Cottage Style

Get away from it all without going on vacation! Turn any home into a dream retreat with these cottage-style decorating ideas. This 216-page book helps you choose your favorite cottage look—whether it's a seaside cottage, a lace-curtained farmhouse, or a chalet in the woods—and provides the tools you need to create the style. Learn how to mix and match colors, furniture, accessories, and treatments for walls, windows, and doors.
$29.95

Garden Style

Wherever you live—in a country cottage, a city apartment, or a suburban house—you can create comfortable, inviting living spaces by blurring the boundaries between indoors and out. This 216-page book shows you how to use garden furnishings, accessories, and ornaments to refresh your home in the garden style. It also includes an extensive list of shops and mail-order sources that can help you achieve this popular look.
$34.95

Garden Style Projects

Create your own quick, affordable accessories, furnishings, and art with this inspiring 168-page book of projects and decorating ideas. Personalize any space with one of 75 projects, including an instant birdbath table, a pebble-roofed birdhouse, a fern-stenciled folding screen, and a twig lamp. Entertain indoors or out with budget-friendly ideas for creating tabletops and party favors as well as topiaries and flower arrangements.
$29.95

Flea Market Decorating

Discover the fun and creativity of decorating with antiques and flea market finds. The key is to look at vintage treasures and secondhand objects with a fresh eye for new purposes they can serve— old rearview mirrors as sconces, cast-iron tub feet as bookends, parachutes as curtains. Beautiful photos in this 224-page book inspire you with hundreds of ideas for repurposing objects. A list of antiques shows and flea markets in the United States, Canada, and Europe point you toward shopping adventures.
$34.95

**Look for these titles wherever quality books
are sold or visit us at bhgbooks.com.**